WHAT DO YOU SEEK?

What Do You Seek?

Encountering the Heart of the Gospel

EDWARD SRI

IGNATIUS PRESS   AUGUSTINE INSTITUTE
San Francisco   Greenwood Village, CO

Cover by Bence Szasz

© 2024 by Edward Sri
All rights reserved
ISBN 978-1-955305-68-6 (HB)
ISBN 978-1-955305-13-6 (PB)
ISBN 978-1-955305-81-5 (eBook)
Library of Congress Control Number 2023949082
Printed in Canada ∞

To all missionaries around the world who
share the Gospel, especially those
who have served in FOCUS.

Contents

Introduction

The Heart of the Gospel

If I wanted to tell you why I love my wife, I wouldn't simply present a list of facts about our relationship: "Edward and Beth met on this date. They were married in Kansas and currently live in Colorado. They have been married over twenty-five years, have had eight children, and have lived in three different houses. They put kids down at night, clean up messes during the day, and drive kids to school in the morning and to various soccer practices in the afternoon. They regularly go for walks, enjoy a date night at least once a month, and enjoy eating fine Italian pastas at home with their family a few times each week."

Though these various details are true and reflect something about our relationship, they don't get to the heart of our love. Instead, if I wanted to tell you why I love my wife, I might describe how we met and fell in love. I'd tell you about her many qualities that initially drew me to her: her intense enthusiasm and zest for life, her ability to listen to and care for others and enter their experience, her love for God and for prayer, her desire to give Jesus her entire heart, and her zeal for evangelization.

I would also share with you the many traits I've grown to appreciate about her, the many things that have made me fall more deeply in love with her as the years have passed. I'd tell you about our amazing children and how much they have brought greater love into our relationship. I'd share with you the various adventures we've experienced along the way, the trials we've faced, the big decisions we've made, and the countless ways we've grown in faith and love together.

In other words, I wouldn't merely list for you *facts* about our relationship. I would tell a story, the story of our love.

The same is true for how I'd introduce someone to the Catholic faith.

If I met someone on a plane and this person asked me why I'm Catholic, why I believe in God, or why I follow Jesus, I wouldn't start with a long list of facts: "Because there are twelve apostles, ten commandments, seven sacraments, three Persons of the Trinity, and one God." I also wouldn't initially focus on a pope in Rome, a priest in my parish, or a Bible on my shelf. I wouldn't zoom in on fasting in Lent, Marian apparitions, or complex moral issues. Of course, I wouldn't avoid these topics if they came up. And, over time, I would hope to discuss them and others, ultimately presenting the fullness of the Catholic faith. But when introducing why I'm Catholic, I wouldn't want to give the impression that the heart of Christianity is the many doctrines we believe, rituals we perform, prayers we recite, saints we remember, and moral codes we follow. To be clear, all these are certainly essential for following Christ. But they do not get to the *heart* of our relationship with him. They do not get to the heart of the Gospel.

Instead, I would initially focus on the greatest love story the world has ever known: the story of God's love for us and of him inviting us into that love. This basic, core story of God's love is known as the Gospel.

All about Love?

Some of you might be taken aback right now: "Wait ... Catholicism is a love story? You've got to be kidding! Of all the religions in the world, Catholicism seems to be the most abstract, ritualistic, impersonal, hierarchical, and complicated. There are so many teachings to believe, rules to adhere to, rituals to perform, and leaders, such as priests, bishops, and the pope, to follow. How could all that possibly be considered a love story?"

I get it. At first glance, being Catholic can appear to be primarily about jumping through a bunch of hoops and checking off an endless series of boxes to make sure you are believing and doing all the right things. For many, it may not seem to be about a relationship of love. In fact, the official summary of our faith—the *Catechism of the Catholic Church*—contains hundreds of pages with nearly three thousand paragraphs, each explaining some doctrine, practice, or moral principle that is essential to living the Catholic faith. To those outside the faith, everything that comprises Catholicism can feel a little overwhelming. But, perhaps even worse, it can also feel quite *underwhelming*: it can seem dry, complicated, boring, impersonal, and abstract. After all, if this is what the essence of the Catholic faith is—a series of doctrines, codes for behavior, and rituals—who would want to give their lives for that? The last thing all those doctrines, rituals, and laws seem to point to is a beautiful love story.

The Gospel: A Love Story?

The earliest Christians, however, didn't seem to have this problem. When those original followers of Jesus shared their faith in Christ with others, what they said captured people's attention. For example, after Saint Peter preached to the crowds on Pentecost, many were cut to the heart and repented. Three thousand people were baptized in a single day! Whatever Peter said worked. Surely, not everyone agreed. And some were even vehemently opposed to what the apostles proclaimed. But, at least from what we find in Acts of the Apostles, no one listening to Peter and the other apostles was bored. No one yawned. Everyone who heard the message they proclaimed was captivated. Some might have been angry. Some might have mocked them. Others were moved to repent and were baptized. But all were drawn in to the dramatic story those apostles told and made a personal decision about how they would respond.

What was it that the apostles proclaimed? First, let's consider what they *didn't* do: They didn't announce a long list of abstract teachings. They didn't focus on apostolic succession, papal infallibility, and transubstantiation. They didn't give everyone lengthy moral instructions about what to do and what behaviors to avoid. They didn't hand out catechisms. Rather, they all told a simple, core message that summarized the story of God's love. Indeed, the apostles' initial proclamation was centered on the Person of Jesus Christ—that Jesus was the Messiah and Lord, the One who fulfilled the prophecies and God's plan for the human family. And he did so by dying on the cross for our sins, rising again on the third day, and ascending to heaven to sit at the right hand of the Father. This basic message of the Gospel—the Good News of Jesus Christ—is known as the kerygma, which is based on the Greek word *kerysso*, meaning "to herald" or "to proclaim". This kerygma was the core message that each of the apostles, as heralds (*kērykes*) of the Gospel, proclaimed to the world.

Their proclamation was simple, concise, and laser focused. Later, the Church needed to expound on this basic, core message of the faith. The writings of Saint Paul and other early Christian leaders, as well as synods and councils of bishops, addressed various challenges and errors that arose in the Christian community. These writings and councils offered crucial clarifications and deeper explanations of the mysteries of the faith. Over time, various teaching documents emerged, such as creeds and decrees from the bishops and popes, that were essential for responding to new questions and challenges to Christianity and for ensuring that God's people maintained the one true faith of the apostles. The *Catechism of the Catholic Church* arose from this tradition and serves as a common reference point for all believers.

All these developments and resources given by the Church were important contributions for ensuring that everything that Jesus handed on to the apostles continued to be passed down faithfully throughout the generations. Following all these teachings remains essential today for being faithful to Jesus Christ. But if we don't know the basic, core message behind all those teachings—the story of God's love and how Jesus Christ brings that story to its climax—the many doctrines, rituals, devotions, and practices of the Catholic faith are less likely to be understood, appreciated, and received fully in our hearts in a way that shapes our entire lives.

First Proclamation

This is why the Catholic Church emphasizes the importance of what it calls "first proclamation"—the first proclamation of the kerygma. Announcing the core Gospel message of God's love and the Person and mission of Jesus Christ is called first proclamation because it is ordinarily meant to come before the more in-depth, systematic presentation of the deeper mysteries of the faith.[1]

---

1   Pontifical Council for the Promotion of the New Evangelization, *Directory for Catechesis* (Washington, DC: United States Conference of Catholic Bishops, 2020), 31–36.

When introducing someone to Christianity, it is usually best to start with the simple message that God loves us, has a plan for our happiness, and wants us to share in his love. And even though we turned away from him in sin, he still seeks us out and wants to be reunited with us. He even became one of us in Jesus Christ and came to forgive us, heal us, and restore us to relationship with the Father. As Pope Francis explained, "On the lips of the catechist the first proclamation must ring out over and over: 'Jesus Christ loves you; he gave his life to save you; and now he is living at your side every day to enlighten, strengthen and free you.' "[2] Knowing this basic outline of the story of God's love, our sin, and his rescuing us—and not just knowing this notionally, but knowing it in a life-transforming way—is a crucial foundation for receiving the many doctrines and deeper aspects of the Catholic faith and integrating them in our daily lives.[3]

Sometimes, however, when we share the faith with others—whether with our children in the home, with friends in the secular world, or with people in the parish—we might dive into the details without making sure the recipients have encountered the foundational message of the kerygma. Perhaps we try to unpack complex topics and the deeper mysteries of the faith before the souls have encountered the Person of Jesus Christ and received the grace of the sacraments.

The same challenge exists for the many Catholics who are baptized, go to Mass on Sundays, and have a familiarity with Catholic teachings but have not said yes to Christ and surrendered their lives to him. If they do not have a personal relationship with Christ—if they have not experienced his

---

2   Pope Francis, apostolic exhortation *Evangelii Gaudium* (Joy of the Gospel) (November 24, 2013), no. 164 (hereafter cited as *EG*).
3   The New Testament has many concise expressions of the Gospel message. See, for example, Mt 1:23; Jn 3:16; 10:10; Acts 10:36; Rom 4:25; 1 Cor 12:3; 15:3; Gal 2:20.

love, his forgiveness, his grace sustaining them—it is harder for them to receive fully the more in-depth, systematic presentation of the faith. Going deeply into complex topics such as the immaculate conception, papal infallibility, the hypostatic union, or contraception with people who have never encountered Jesus Christ in a personal, life-shaping way is not likely to be fruitful.

This doesn't mean we have to put off all systematic catechesis in our Catholic schools, in our various parish faith formation efforts, and in our families until we are absolutely sure those we are trying to reach have had a conversion. An organic and systematic presentation of the faith is still essential for catechesis. But we should be aware that the ideal process of initially sharing the first proclamation of the Gospel may not have taken place yet. So we should do all we can to evangelize, facilitate a deeper encounter with Christ, and consistently bring everything back to the kerygma. No matter what we are presenting about the Catholic faith, we should not simply teach the truth of a particular doctrine but should also present that truth in a way that inspires a deeper conversion, always teaching in a way that inspires souls to yield their lives more fully to Jesus Christ.[4]

---

4 See John Paul II, apostolic exhortation *Catechesi Tradendae* (On Catechesis in Our Time) (October 16, 1979), nos. 19–20 (hereafter cited as *CT*). "But in catechetical practice, this model order must allow for the fact that the initial evangelization has often not taken place." Many of the faithful who have been baptized and received the sacraments and a systematic catechesis "still remain hesitant for a long time about committing their whole lives to Jesus Christ.... This means that 'catechesis' must often concern itself not only with nourishing and teaching the faith, but also with arousing it unceasingly with the help of grace, with opening the heart, with converting, and with preparing total adherence to Jesus Christ on the part of those who are still on the threshold of faith." (*CT* 19). A similar point is made by the Pontifical Council for the Promotion of the New Evangelization: "If it is still useful to make conceptual distinctions between *pre-evangelization, first proclamation, catechesis, ongoing formation,* in the present context, it is no longer possible to stress such differences. In fact, on the one hand those today who ask for or have already received the grace of the sacraments often do not have an explicit experience of faith or do not intimately know its power and

The reason this is so important is that once someone has
received the first proclamation of the Gospel and responded
by saying yes to Christ in his life—once he has experienced how friendship with Jesus makes all the difference
in his life—then the other aspects of the faith will make
more sense and be more integrated in the way he views the
world and the way he lives. Without the integration of
the Gospel, the various truths of the faith may seem like
abstract teachings—something a person might agree to but
not something that shapes his entire life. This is why the
Church in recent decades has called for a New Evangelization: a re-presentation of the Gospel to those who may be
baptized but have not yet encountered Christ in a personal
way. Many practicing Catholics might know some facts
about Jesus and the Catholic faith, but they have not personally said yes to him, abandoning their lives to him.[5] They
are shaped more by the secular culture around them than by
the Word of God. They might be baptized, go to Mass, and
even volunteer at the parish, but they have adopted a secular
model of thinking and living.[6] Though they go through the
motions of the faith, they live their daily lives in a way that
is far removed from the Gospel. These souls do not simply
need further in-depth theology. They need more than that.
They need the foundations. They need a truly Christian
lens for seeing their lives. They need to encounter the love,
mercy, and grace of Jesus Christ in a life-transforming way.

warmth; on the other, a formal proclamation limited to the bare enunciation of the concepts
of the faith would not permit an understanding of the faith itself, which is instead a new
horizon of life that is opened wide, starting from the encounter with the Lord Jesus.... The
proclamation [of the Gospel] can therefore no longer be considered simply the first stage of
faith, preliminary to catechesis, but rather the essential dimension of every moment of catechesis." *Directory for Catechesis*, 56–57.

5   "This yes to Jesus Christ contains two dimensions: trustful abandonment to God (*fides
qua*) and loving assent to all that he has revealed to us (*fides quae*)." Pontifical Council for the
Promotion of the New Evangelization, *Directory for Catechesis*, 18; see also *CT* 20.

6   John Paul II, *Redemptoris Missio* (December 7, 1990), no. 33.

They need to experience how friendship with Christ makes all the difference in their lives.

In sum, they need the Gospel.

Christocentric Catechesis

The passing on of the faith is meant to be Christocentric— centered on Jesus Christ. Everything the Catholic Church teaches is, in the end, all about the love of Jesus. Whether it is about saints, sacraments, Holy Week, holy water, or moral teachings, everything we believe comes from God, who is love (see 1 Jn 4:8) and who freely chose to create us out of love because he wanted to share his love with us. And even though we turned away from his love in sin, he still pursues us, longing to be one with us again. Out of love, he even entered our world and became one of us in Jesus Christ and died for us so that we can be reunited with him. Every detail about the Catholic faith is ultimately from that story of God's amazing love for us and about our sharing in that love and being trans- formed by it. Whether we're a priest giving a homily, a director of religious education leading OCIA, or a parent teaching a child, we should regularly connect whatever we are presenting about the faith to that larger story of God's amazing love for us, known as the Gospel.

Unfortunately, many Catholics today either do not know the basic outline of the Gospel message or are not confident sharing it with others. The kerygma is not second nature for many of us, like it was for Saint Peter and the apostles. So, while there are many Catholic resources that expound on the various doctrines of the Catholic faith, this book focuses on the kerygma—that basic, core Gospel message that is at the foundation of everything we believe and do and are as Catholics.

The Gospel message can be presented in various ways. In this book, I will build upon the general five-part outline used by priests, parish leaders, and ordinary laypeople in a missionary organization I've been blessed to be a part of. The five parts of the kerygma can be seen summarized with five *R*s:[7]

Relationship: God created us out of love and for love. We are made for relationship with him.

Rebellion: We turned away from God in sin and now find ourselves fallen, wounded, captured by the enemy, and separated from God.

Reconciliation: Even though we sinned, God still seeks us out. He became one of us and offered his life as a gift of love on our behalf so that we could be reconciled with him.

Re-creation: God doesn't just want to forgive us. He wants to make each of us "a new creation" (2 Cor 5:17), healing and changing our hearts to love like he loves. He does this work of transformation through his Church.

Response: Jesus invites us to respond to the Gospel and follow him.

Again, there are many other ways to summarize the Gospel message. This is just one approach—one that has been easily and effectively used in parishes, families, and communities across the country and by people of all walks of life: bishops, priests, deacons, religious sisters, lay leaders in the parish, Catholic schoolteachers, moms and dads, young adults, and college students. The points expressed by these five *R*s not only come from the heart of the Catholic tradition but also

7   These "5 R's" have been used by various parish and campus missionaries in FOCUS. See, Curtis Martin and Edward Sri, eds., *Foundations in Discipleship* (Huntington, IN: Our Sunday Visitor, 2021), pp. 40–51, 202–11.

are easy for laypeople to remember and reproduce in parish, family, and workplace settings.

Whatever method or resource we use to communicate the kerygma, it is important that we come back to this first proclamation of the Gospel countless times whenever we are passing on the Catholic faith. It's not something we present only once. It's something we bring up over and over, connecting whatever aspect of the faith we are focusing on to the foundational big picture of God's love. As Pope Francis explained, "This first proclamation is called 'first' not because it exists at the beginning and can then be forgotten or replaced by other more important things. It is first in a qualitative sense because it is the principal proclamation, the one which we must hear again and again in different ways, the one which we must announce one way or another throughout the process of catechesis, at every level and moment."[8]

And this is true not only for our sharing the faith with others. *It's also crucial for our own friendship with the Lord.* For the story of God's love for us is not merely a story from the past, nor is it a story that we need to hear only once. It's a story that we need to ponder anew throughout our lives. God is constantly inviting us ever deeper into the story of his love. He thirsts for us. He always wants to share even more of his love for us, and he longs for our hearts to grow in our love for him in return. Just as I grow in my love for my wife through the various twists and turns in the story our marriage, so we are always being invited deeper into the story of God's love throughout the journey of our lives—always being invited to new ways to trust him more, surrender to him more, serve him more. This is why our own faith formation must always lead us to an ever-deeper interiorization of the kerygma. As Pope Francis explained, "We must not think that in catechesis the kerygma

---

8   *EG* 164.

gives way to a supposedly more 'solid' formation. Nothing is more solid, profound, secure, meaningful and wisdom-filled than that initial proclamation. All Christian formation consists of entering more deeply into the kerygma."[9]

That's what this book aims to do: help you enter more deeply into the Gospel. This book is not so much a tool to help you share the Gospel with others. There are already many resources for that.[10] Instead, this book is more for you: to help you interiorize the Gospel and go deeper into the kerygma. It is a prayerful reflection on the key aspects of the Gospel message. The aim is to help you ponder the mysteries of God's love for you and his work of salvation—not just to understand the Gospel intellectually but to interiorize it in your heart, to integrate it more in your daily life, and to prayerfully consider the ways Jesus is inviting you to take that next step in your relationship with him. For a true disciple is always on the look-out for new ways to welcome Christ ever more in his heart. And the more we ourselves are continuously being transformed by the kerygma, the more we will radiate the joy of the Gospel to the world around us.

9   *EG* 165.
10   See, for example, Curtis Martin and Edward Sri, eds., *Foundations for Discipleship*; Curtis Martin, *Making Missionary Disciples: How to Live the Method Modeled by the Master* (Genesee, CO: FOCUS, 2018); Fr. John Riccardo, *Rescued: The Unexpected and Extraordinary News of the Gospel* (Ann Arbor, MI: Word Among Us, 2020). There are also free resources on how to share the Gospel with others available at focusequip.org.

Section One

Signs of the Gospel

You have made us for Yourself, and our hearts are restless until they rest in You.

—Saint Augustine, *Confessions*, 1, 1.

Chapter 1

"Seek and You Will Find"

Do you know the very first words Jesus spoke to his two orig-inal disciples?

Think of all the things Jesus could have said to them in that initial encounter. He could have talked about the importance of prayer or the Ten Commandments. He could have taught them the Our Father or the Sermon on the Mount.

He could have been very direct, calling them to repent, turn away from sin, and accept the kingdom of God. Or he simply could have told them how much God loved them and wanted to forgive them, heal them, and be in relationship with them.

Instead, Jesus focused on something else. He didn't talk about important ideas like these. Not yet. Rather, he zoomed in on their hearts. He wanted them to pause for a moment and retreat from the busyness, burdens, cares, and distractions of daily life and take a moment to do something most people rarely take time to do: look inside. To look inside their hearts and pay attention to what was there. It was as if he knew they would not be fully ready to hear the Gospel message he came to offer until they looked inward and became more aware of the deeper stirrings in their souls. So, before he addressed any of those other important topics—and even before he invited them to follow him and learn more about him—he asked them a very personal question, a question of the heart. He asked them, "What do you seek?" (Jn 1:38).

It seems Jesus knew that if they looked inside their hearts and considered what they were really seeking in life, they might be better prepared to encounter him and receive all that he wanted to offer them. So he invited them to look inside.

How about you? Do you take time to look inside your heart and consider what's really there? Most of us are too busy and too distracted, running from one appointment to the next, one amusement to the next, one click on our devices to the next. Or, if we ever do have a moment alone, in stillness, in silence, with our own thoughts, we feel uncomfortable. We might even panic. We're afraid to sit with ourselves in the void. So we quickly distract ourselves. We turn on some music, watch a show, do a chore, perform a task, or pull out our phones to distract ourselves. Many of us mainly live on the surface of our lives. We are existing. We might be getting a lot of things done. We might even have fun on occasion. But where is this all going? And are we really living life to the full? How can we be if we don't even take time to become aware of the motions in our hearts?

That's why Jesus wants those words he spoke to those disciples two thousand years ago to reverberate through the centuries and come to us today. Indeed, Jesus stands before us now, inviting us to look inside. He's asking us the same personal question: "What do you seek?"

But here we must be clear: this is not merely an intellectual question. Jesus is not looking for us to give an abstract answer on a theology quiz (*Quiz Question:* What do you seek? *Correct Answer:* peace, happiness, God). Rather, Jesus is inviting us to take an honest look inside, to examine our hearts and consider what it is that we're *really* seeking ... right now. Indeed, this question is like an examination of conscience: *What am I really trying to find my happiness in: a certain job, a certain relationship, a certain opportunity, a certain achievement? What am*

I grasping for that I think I must absolutely have in order to be fulfilled? What am I anxiously clinging to, afraid that if I don't have it, I will lose my security or be alone, unseen, and unknown? Where am I seeking my identity and confidence in life: a bigger salary, success, status, acceptance, approval, praise? More friends, more control, more comfort, more stuff?

Whether we're new to the Christian vision or have been devout believers for many years, this basic question of Jesus—"What do you seek?"—is one we must seriously reflect on over and over throughout our lives. Jesus wants us regularly to renew our encounter with him. And the first step toward this encounter could be prayerfully imagining Jesus looking you in the eye and asking you to peer inside your heart and take an honest look at what you notice there. He asks you, "What do you seek?"

Signposts

There was one famous leader in ancient Rome who, by all standards of his time, had it all. He had one of the sharpest minds in the world and was a gifted orator. He leaped from one success to another. He received many praises and honors, achieved great fame, and rose to one of the highest, most coveted positions in the Roman Empire. On top of all that, he also had a robust social life full of friendships, entertainment, fine food, drink, women, and pleasure. On the outside, it appeared he had everything he needed to be happy.

But on the inside, something was missing. All the wealth, honors, and pleasures of this world did not satisfy the deepest desires of his heart. He was still longing for something more. But what made this famous man different from many others is that he actually dared to look inside his heart and consider the question, "What do you seek?" The more he paid attention to the movements in his heart, the more he became aware of a deeper desire that nothing in this world could satisfy. No amount of praise, power, sex, or money could ever bring him the peace, security, and union with others he was seeking. He eventually came to realize that this ongoing, deep desire in his heart was pointing to something beyond this world: it was pointing to God. Only later in life, after many failed attempts at finding lasting happiness, did this successful man, who went on to become known as the great Saint Augustine, finally direct those deepest yearnings in his soul toward the One to whom they were ultimately pointing. And only then could he famously write this prayer to God: "Our hearts are restless until they rest in you."

What Do You Seek?

When I was a professor teaching Introduction to Theology to college freshmen, I sometimes asked them a series of questions that all came down to the same fundamental question Jesus asked: "What do you seek?"

You can imagine my dialogue with a student in class going something like this:

What do you seek?

Uh, what do you mean? This week? Right now?

Sure.

Well, I've got a midterm exam in my history class tomorrow. I hope I get a good grade.

Why?

Well, doesn't everyone want a good grade? I need to pass the class.

And why do you want to pass the class?

(He laughs.) It's a required class in the core curriculum. I need it to graduate!

Why do you want to graduate?

(He laughs again.) So I can get a job.

And why do you want a job?

To make money, of course.... Are you going to ask me why I want money?

Yes.

(He laughs yet again.) Well, obviously I need money to buy things, to get stuff, to go out with my friends.

Why do you want that?

That's what people do!

But is there anything more?

Well, I'll eventually need money to buy a house and provide for a family.

Why do you want that?

I don't want to live life alone. I'd like to have a family someday.

Okay. But why?

I don't know. I just want to be happy.

This line of questioning usually got a little awkward after about the third or fourth round. But it always ended right there with happiness. And it always grabbed the students' attention and made an important point. Too often in life, we are constantly running after one thing and then the next, feeling pressure to succeed, find new relationships, gain new experiences, and make it to the next level. But we rarely stop to ask why we are doing all that we are doing. Where is all this going? What is the ultimate goal we are aiming for? For many years, though this line of questioning in the classroom took many different directions, it always led, in the end, to the same answer: we are seeking happiness.

Underneath all our various pursuits in life is the deepest desire we all possess: to be happy. And that happiness is found in God alone. As the *Catechism of the Catholic Church* (*CCC*) explains, God created us with "longings for the infinite and for happiness" (33). Realizing this makes all the difference in life. We are created with infinite desires, and nothing in this world will ever be able to satisfy us—no amount of praise, success, fame, money, or pleasure. We tell ourselves, *I just want X,* and we convince ourselves we will finally be fulfilled if we get it. But once we obtain it, it's never enough. We want more. More of whatever X is. Or when we realize X is not enough, we turn our attention to the next thing on the horizon that we think will give us the fulfillment we're looking for.

Realizing this truth about our infinite desires is crucial. And we need to grasp it not just in our heads but at the core of our being. If I'm not convinced that in all my desiring I am really desiring God, then I will, inevitably, keep pouring out my life in things that will never satisfy. I will keep trying to get that next title, possession, honor, or relationship that I think will make me happy. If I fall short, I will try again. And if I discover I can't get what I'm looking for, I will turn my attention to something else that I hope will give me that security, peace, and fulfillment I desire—a new friend group, success, a new fun adventure, pleasure. Yet, even if I get all these things, I still will be left unsatisfied. My heart was made for something more. I have infinite desires. And only the Infinite One can satisfy the deepest desires of my heart.

Questioning Creatures

When reading a beautiful reflection by the sixteenth-century Spanish Carmelite Saint John of the Cross, we are invited to consider what we might do when something happens in our lives and we become more aware of our soul's deeper longings. We feel a hurt, an ache, a hole in our hearts. Only God can fill that hole. But most of us turn to things and people of this world to fill the void. So we set off on a journey to seek our heart's desire. We begin questioning creatures—the things God has made—asking them if they have seen "the one I love most". They honestly tell us they are not what we are looking for but that he "passed these groves in haste", "pouring out a thousand graces" and clothing his creatures with beauty.

John of the Cross explains that God created all things with "some trace of who he is ... by endowing them with innumerable graces and qualities, making them beautiful".[1] The point is this: what draws us to delight in the goodness of a certain friend, a glass of wine; a good grade, or a significant accomplishment—or the beauty of a sunset, a piece of music, or a certain person we find ourselves attracted to—is ultimately something of God's own goodness and beauty. In other words, *it is God whom we ultimately seek.* The creatures themselves cannot fill the void in our hearts. They can only point to the One who can.

John of the Cross says that our souls have "infinite caverns". At the center of our lives are "deep caverns of the soul", and "nothing less than the infinite will fill them."[2] There is nothing wrong with pursuing good things in this world. We just don't want to place them at the center. As one commentator on John of the Cross explains, seeking God at the center of all we do allows us to pursue the good things of this world with the proper order and peace. But when we grasp after something less than God in the hopes it will fulfill us, we will end up with frustration, anxiety, emptiness, and discord. We cannot put our dreams on par with God. We cannot seek God *and* X at the same level. That would be to make an idol of whatever we are seeking. We must be willing to seek first the

---

1 St. John of the Cross, *The Spiritual Canticle*, in *The Collected Works of St. John of the Cross*, trans. Kieran Cavanaugh, O.C.D., and Otilio Rodriguez, O.C.D. (Washington, DC: ICS Publications, 1991), 5, 1.

2 St. John of the Cross, *Living Flame of Love*, 3, 18, 22, quoted in Iain Matthew, *The Impact of God: Soundings from St. John of the Cross* (London: Hodder & Stoughton, 1995), p. 27.

kingdom of God and trust that all other things will be pro-
vided by God as we need (see Mt 6:25–34). "When people,
things, events are loved *within God*, there is harmony. When
they get set alongside God—'set in a balance with God'—a
process is begun in which affectivity groans under the violence
it is inflicting on itself."[3]

We can pray to God about the things that get in the way
of our seeking God first: our desire to achieve, to stand out,
to control, to manage, to seek approval, to seek acceptance, to
seek praise, to seek more for ourselves. We can say to God,
"I don't need it, not because it is bad, but because it is bad at
the center, and I want You at the center." We can continue,
"I do not need to do these things, not because they are necessarily wrong, but because I need You, and when I have shown
myself that it is You I really want, then I can return to these
others free, not as a slave."[4]

Late Have I Loved You

Saint Augustine similarly imagines himself questioning all the
good things in God's creation to see whether they are the fulfillment of all his desires. They reply, "We are not God. Seek
what is above us.... God is he who made us."[5] They have
reflections of the truth, goodness, and beauty of God, but it is
God himself whom Augustine ultimately seeks.

It was coming to this realization that all his desiring was, in
the end, a desiring for God that led Augustine to lament that
he had not arrived at this conclusion sooner and had spent
so much of his life restlessly seeking happiness in the things
God had made instead of in God himself. At the same time,

---

3   Matthew, *Impact of God*, 40–41.
4   Matthew, *Impact of God*, 43.
5   Augustine, *Confessions*, 10, 6.

Augustine expressed gratitude that God pierced through his deafness, called him out of his darkness, and drew Augustine back to himself. Augustine prayed the following prayer, to which most of us can relate:

Too late have I loved you, O Beauty so ancient, O Beauty so new.

Too late have I loved you! You were within me but I was outside myself, and there I sought you!

In my weakness, I ran after the beauty of the things you have made.

You were with me, and I was not with you.

The things you have made kept me from you—the things which would have no being unless they existed in you!

You have called, you have cried, and you have pierced my deafness.

You have radiated forth, you have shined out brightly, and you have dispelled my blindness.

You have sent forth your fragrance, and I have breathed it in, and I long for you.

I have tasted you, and I hunger and thirst for you.

You have touched me, and I ardently desire your peace.[6]

Reflection Questions:

1. When you look at the modern world, what are the things you see people pursuing to find their happiness? Why will those things, even if they're not bad, fail to satisfy the desires of their hearts?

---

6   Augustine, *Confessions*, 10, https://melbournecatholic.org/news/late-have-i-loved-you-st -augustine#:~:text=Prayer%20of%20Saint%20Augustine,the%20things%20you%20 have%20made. Accessed February 19, 2023.

2. Now take an honest look inside your own heart. What are the things you seek in order to find happiness, identity, and security?

3. Jesus said, "Seek first [God's] kingdom" (Mt 6:33). What would your life look like if you truly sought God first? What is one thing you can do to seek God first more?

Chapter 2

Lord, I Need You

Put yourself in this woman's situation: She had a physical ailment that would not go away. For twelve years she suffered, feeling life continuously going out of her, as constant weakness and fatigue usually accompanied her condition. The hardest part, however, was not the physical pain she endured. It was the isolation she felt. In her culture, her particular malady came with a severe social stigma. She could not come in close contact with others. Had she tried, she would have been ostracized. She, therefore, likely spent twelve long years alone: No friendships. No community. No sense of belonging.

We can imagine her desperation: *Where is my life going? Will this ever get better? Why is this happening? Is there any point to my life?*

She had tried everything in her power to fix her problem. She even spent all her money on many physicians—either doctors who charged exorbitant fees for the wealthy or quacks taking advantage of the poor in desperate situations like hers. Whatever the case may be, she was no better as a result. In fact, these so-called physicians only made her worse.

But there was more: Though she probably had been living on some inherited money that helped make ends meet, all that money was now gone, and she found herself in a most dangerous situation. Not only was she isolated socially and worse off physically, but financially, she was not even able to provide for herself anymore. The last penny was gone. What was she to do?

This woman, of course, is the hemorrhaging woman the Gospels tell us about.[1] We don't know if she was particularly religious. One could understand if she wondered how God could allow people like her to suffer as she did. Maybe she was a sincere believer and hung on to her faith through it all. But whatever the case may be, whatever faith she might have had was being tested like never before: Did she really believe in a God who loved her and was the absolute foundation of her life? Did she believe in a God who works everything for good, even in this most desperate of situations?

We don't know where she was in her spiritual life, but the reality of hitting rock bottom seems to have made her aware of an important truth: *how much she was not in control.*

She had tried and tried to make things better on her own. But nothing worked. She couldn't change her situation. She couldn't stop the bleeding. She couldn't get the physicians to heal her. She couldn't make the people in her community treat her differently. She couldn't force people to accept her and live in friendship with her.

She had tried doing everything she could to bring an end to the pain and loneliness, but she had finally hit a wall. She was incapable of changing anything. She felt completely weak, vulnerable, and powerless. She knew beyond a doubt that she was not in control. All she could do now was make a choice: Should she continue to try to fix her problem on her own, as if more plotting, planning, willpower, determination, and doctor visits might finally make things better? Or should she accept that she cannot change everything, that she needs something greater than herself, that she needs God? Should

---

1   See Mt 9:20–22; Mk 5:25–34; Lk 8:43–48.

she surrender it all to God and entrust her life entirely into his hands?

What choice did she make? She chose the latter. When Jesus was passing by, she reached out, touched just the fringe of his garments, and was healed. What no amount of money, no amount of effort, no amount of care from the doctors could do over the last twelve years, Jesus did in an instant. But it was only when she came to him at this lowest point, in utter humility, recognizing the truth about herself and her complete dependence on God for everything. It was only when she reached out to him to do what she'd realized she could never do on her own that God stepped into her life in the most powerful way and she was changed.

I Am Not My Savior

The Gospel can't be received as good news until we realize how desperately we need it. Imagine hearing the news that scientists found a cure for a certain rare, life-threatening disease. That might be good to know, and you might be thankful for this new medical advance, but you would not experience it as good news in a deeply personal way unless you or someone you love happened to suffer from that rare disease.

Similarly, souls who are not aware of their grave situation—of how much they need the Divine Physician—might not be ready to appreciate the Christian Gospel message for what it really is: not just *good* news but the most amazing news in all the world and something we all most urgently need. I must realize how sick I am before I can fully appreciate going to the doctor.

This is why God often uses circumstances in our lives to wake us up, to help us see reality clearly, to come to a deeper awareness of the truth about ourselves: that we are not in control. Not that God himself is the cause of our suffering. As we will see later in this book, we, through sin, brought suffering into this world, and we all will have our share in suffering. But God can bring good out of difficult circumstances and even turn the trials in our lives into opportunities to grow and be blessed in new ways. These circumstances may be painful situations that we realize we cannot change. It could be a health issue, a lost job, a lost relationship, a lost opportunity. It could be the way our boss treats us, a troubled marriage, the choices one of our children makes, or a feeling of being not noticed, not accepted, left out, and alone. We keep doing all we can to change the situation, but nothing works. We are not in control.

These circumstances might be wounds from our past. Perhaps we were born with a disability, our parents divorced, we experienced some kind of trauma or abuse, we made some bad decisions we cannot take back, or we fell into an addiction that we still battle today. As much as we wish we were beyond it all, these hurts from our past continue to affect us in the present. And there seems to be nothing we can do to change it.

These circumstances may also be personal struggles we face today. Maybe there's something we don't like about ourselves: a bad habit, a deep insecurity, a way of relating to others, or even a sin that we can't get rid of. We keep bringing the same weakness to Confession but notice little improvement. No matter how hard we try, we simply cannot change.

God sometimes uses the difficult circumstances of our lives to help us know more profoundly the truth about ourselves: how little in control we really are and how much we are dependent on him, for everything. In those low points of life, we come to know more fully—not just in our heads but experientially, in the depth of our being—a foundational truth we should be in touch with *all* the time. It's the truth Jesus revealed about our lives at the Last Supper: "Apart from me you can do nothing" (Jn 15:5). So, when we experience how we simply cannot change a painful event from the past, a challenging situation in the present, other people, or even ourselves, we become more open to receiving the fullness of the good news God always offers us.

Strength in the Lord

Here, we can think about Saint Augustine again. He was a man longing for freedom. Before his conversion, Augustine had been trying to liberate himself from his sexual sins. He had experienced the emptiness of this way of life and sincerely wanted to change. But his habits, forged over many years from the time of his youth, were too strong. His attraction to those pleasures had a significant hold on him. No matter how hard he tried, he simply could not let them go.

Augustine even envisioned his passions tormenting him, saying, "Are you going to dismiss us? From this moment we shall never be with you again, for ever and ever. From this moment you will never again be allowed to do this thing or that, for ever more.... Do you think you can live without these things?"[2] Hesitant to make a firm break with his sexual sins, he kept putting off his decision, famously praying, "Give me chastity ... but not yet."[3] He was in agony, desiring to change, but lamenting his inability to do so. He cried out, "How long shall I go on saying 'tomorrow, tomorrow'? Why not now? Why not make an end of my ugly sins at this moment?"[4]

It was in the midst of this long inner struggle that Augustine learned of other people who had made the leap to Christianity. They had given up their unchaste lifestyles and committed

---

2   Augustine, *Confessions*, 8, 11.
3   Augustine, *Confessions*, 8, 7.
4   Augustine, *Confessions*, 8, 12.

themselves to Christ. What was most surprising to Augustine was the fact that these people were much less educated, less famous, less impressive than he. How were they able to take the courageous step and turn their lives around while he, the great Augustine, could not let go of his sexual sins? He was ashamed that he did not have the strength to do what these simple men had done.

Augustine described how, at this moment, he could envision the beautiful virtue of continence (self-control) calling out to him, reminding him that it was not by their own strength that these people were able to change. It was all by the grace of God. These men and women had found freedom from their sins and had been transformed because they learned to rely on God and not themselves. And that same grace was available to him. Augustine envisioned the virtue of continence saying to him, "Can you not do what these men and these women do? Do you think they find the strength to do it in themselves and not in the Lord their God? It was the Lord their God who gave me to them. Why do you try to stand in your own strength and fail? Cast yourself upon God and have no fear. He will not shrink away and let you fall. Cast yourself upon him without fear, for he will welcome you and cure you of all your ills."[5]

This was the crucial turning point for Augustine. It was not that he suddenly came up with more willpower, more self-control on his own. He didn't discover five new ways to overcome addiction or a sure-fire plan to grow in one virtue each week during Lent that would lead him to freedom from sexual sin by Easter. No. It was that he hit this low point in his life, experienced his utter weakness and inability to change, and then, in humility, turned to God, begging the Lord to help him. It was when Augustine finally came to terms with how

5   Augustine, *Confessions*, 8, 11.

little he could do on his own and how much he depended on God that he began to learn to rely on God's grace. And he was transformed.

How about you? Is there an area of your life where you feel like the woman in the Gospel: powerless, afraid, alone? Or do you have an area where you feel like Augustine: unable to change no matter how hard you try and relying on yourself and not on God? If so, this may be a part of you that God is inviting you to surrender to him and allow him to do what you cannot do on your own. But how does one go about entrusting his life to God in this way? That's what we will begin to consider next.

Reflection Questions:

1 Can you relate to the example of Saint Augustine and his inability to overcome his particular weakness? How so?
2. How did Augustine eventually experience change?
3. What is an area of your life where you feel as if you do not have control—for example, a relationship, a situation, a weakness you can't change? What can you do to entrust that area of your life to God, to surrender it to him and rely on his power to do what you cannot do on your own?

Section Two

The Gospel in Five Parts

Thus the tempter was outwitted
By a wisdom deeper still:
Remedy and ailment fitted,
Means to cure and means to kill;
That the world might be acquitted,
Christ would do his Father's will.

— "Crux Fidelis",
traditional Good Friday hymn
from The Roman Missal

Chapter 3

Part 1: Relationship— You Were Chosen

I'll never forget holding my first child. We were at the hospital, Beth had just delivered our baby girl, and the nurse handed her to me. It seemed surreal. I had held babies before, but this was different. This wasn't just me holding a baby; this was me holding *my* baby. I was a first-time dad. This was my daughter, and I was holding my own child for the very first time!

I was in awe over this experience of fatherhood. Even though my baby could not yet talk, gesture, or write, I experienced a profound connection with her, especially in that first week of her life. Newborns often have their eyes closed, but one time, after she woke up in the middle of the night, I was holding her in our living room, and her eyes suddenly opened. For the first time, she was just staring into my eyes. This had never happened before. I found myself gazing into her eyes while she gazed back into mine. That mutual gaze held for what seemed like hours, and I was suddenly overcome by a love I had never experienced before—the love of a father for a child. I couldn't hold back. I repeatedly said to her, "Oh, I love you!... Oh, I love you!"

As I look back on that experience, what I find fascinating is that my daughter didn't do anything to earn my love. My four-day-old baby didn't vacuum the living room, wash the dishes, or mow the lawn. On that night, she didn't produce good grades, win scholarships, or achieve success in a career. Nor did she win my heart by behaving well, giving me hugs, or paying me compliments. She was just an infant. Still, I was overcome with love. It was enough that she simply existed, that she was my daughter—and I delighted in her.

Our heavenly Father looks at us the same way. At the foundation of Christianity is the Good News of our heavenly Father's love, a love that goes far beyond any purely human love we may experience. The divine love is so much more. It is not a love that lets us down. It is not a love with any strings attached; it is not performance based. It is not a love that we can earn. It is freely given. It can only be received.

In the Father's eyes, it is good that we exist. Even when we make mistakes. Even when we are not at our best. Even when we turn away from him. His love for us never pulls back. Unlike most human loves, the divine love gives completely and never stops, no matter what we do. It is a love that remains with us and delights in us, even when we fall and are far from perfect.

But it is also a love that constantly calls out to us, inviting us to listen to the deepest desires of our souls, beckoning us to turn away from sin and turn back to him, and drawing us out of the messes we often make with our lives so that we can walk in his ways, follow his plan, and share ever more in his abundant life.

Most of all, as free and unconditional as God's love is, he nevertheless longs for our response. He stands at the door and knocks. He does not force his way into our souls, but he yearns for us to open the door of our hearts and give ourselves to him in return. It's as if he is overcome with love and looks into our eyes, saying, "Oh, I love you ... Oh, I love you!" And he ardently awaits our response. Indeed, this unfathomable divine love, which is so far beyond even the best of human loves, is not just what we were made for. It's what brought us into existence in the first place.

"It Was Very Good"

To appreciate this crucial point, we're going to walk through a few basic details from the very beginning of the Bible, in the book of Genesis. Even if you've heard these points before, I invite you to ponder them anew. They are so foundational to the Gospel message that God wants us to reflect on them throughout our lives in order to come to know and appreciate his love at ever-deeper levels.

First, let's consider what the biblical account of Creation tells us about how God really sees us. You may already be familiar with the basics of the story: After creating the sun, moon, and stars, God saw that "it was good" (1:18). After creating the birds and fish, he pondered his creation again and saw that "it was good" (1:21). And after bringing the beasts of the field into existence, God once again looked upon what he had made and saw that "it was good" (1:25).

But have you ever noticed how after he created man and woman—the crowning of his creation—something different happened? In awe over his supreme achievement, God didn't just see that "it was good." He rejoiced over man and woman and saw that "it was *very* good" (1:31, emphasis added).

Now let's make that line personal: "It was very good." Let's see that line as not just about creation and humanity in general, but specifically about *you*. Imagine God looking at you. Imagine God looking at all you've done, all you've said, all your thoughts, all your hopes, all your desires, and saying, "You are very good." How would you feel?

You know yourself. If you're like most people, you probably realize you have many shortcomings. Fears. Mistakes.

Weaknesses. Failures. Sins. You know you are far from perfect. And yet here is the amazing truth: God still delights in you and wants to share his life with you. God sees you and says, "You are very good."

This doesn't mean you don't have areas you need to work on. As we will see, God is calling all of us to repent and turn away from whatever faults and sins keep us from union with him. But that doesn't take away from his fundamental, steadfast love for us, and the goodness of being made in his image (*CCC* 2566). Our imperfections may be significant, but they don't have to define us. The Father's infinite love for us and his desire to heal and transform us are greater than any of our sins. As Saint John Paul II explained, "We are not the sum of our weaknesses and failures; we are the sum of the Father's love for us and our real capacity to become the image of his Son."[1]

Out of Love, for Love

Second, let's consider *why* God created us. The most astonishing aspect of his creating us is that he didn't *have* to do this. God didn't need us. Yet he freely *chose* to create us! Consider this remarkable passage from the opening paragraph of the *Catechism*, which underscores how profound it is that God chose to bring us into existence:

> God, infinitely perfect and blessed in himself, in a plan of sheer goodness freely created man to make him share in his own blessed life. (*CCC* 1)

Take a moment to ponder this important truth the *Catechism* alludes to here: *we did not have to exist.* Pause right now,

---

1   John Paul II, Homily at the 17th World Youth Day (Toronto, Ontario, July 28, 2002).

close your eyes for a few moments, and feel the weight of that: God didn't have to create us. If God didn't choose to create us, we would not be here. He did not *need* to bring us into existence. He's God, after all, and is "infinitely perfect and blessed in himself". Yet, for some reason, he still freely *chose* to create us. But why? That's the crucial question we must consider: If God didn't need us, why would he want to bring us into existence?

The answer? *Because of love.*

As the *Catechism* says, God freely chose to bring us into existence so that we could "share in his own blessed life". As the thirteenth-century theologian Saint Bonaventure explained, God created all things not to increase his own glory but to share it with others.[2] "For God has no other reason for creating than his love and goodness" (*CCC* 293).

What a beautiful point we should always remember! The God who is love—the God who is "infinitely perfect and blessed in himself"—freely chose to create us so that he could share his love with us! Indeed, we were created out of love, and we were created for love. In a sense, we might say we were *loved* into existence.

Out of love, God created us to share his life with us so that we could live in friendship with him. Indeed, as the *Catechism* goes on to explain, God longs for us. He thirsts for us—for our time, attention, love. How remarkable it is that Almighty God, who is "infinitely perfect and blessed in himself", desires to share his love with us. This is the whole point of creating us: so that he can live in relationship with us.

Mother Teresa absolutely marveled over this mystery. She was in awe over how the God of the universe loves us so much that he longs for our love in return: "That God is high, transcendent, all-powerful, almighty, I can understand that

---

2   *CCC* 293, citing St. Bonaventure, *In II Sent.* I, 2, 2, 1.

because I am so small. But that God has become small, and
that he thirsts for my love, begs for it—I *cannot* understand it,
I *cannot* understand it, I *cannot* understand it!"[3]

"God Loves Everyone" versus "God Loves Me"

Notice how what blew Mother Teresa's mind wasn't just
God's love for the human family in general but his love specifically for her, personally.

Growing up Catholic, I had often heard the basic message, "God loves you." But this fundamental point did not
move me like it did Mother Teresa. Not at all. Sure, I believed
that God loves me, but it was not something that seemed very
important. I can remember thinking, *Yes, I know God loves
me. What's the big deal? That seems rather basic. God loves everyone. I'm a part of "everyone". So of course God loves me.*

It was only later in my young adult years that I came to
encounter God's love on a much more *personal* level—and it
changed everything in my life. I had been a practicing Catholic.
I went to Mass, said some prayers, and tried to be a good person. I tried to believe the right things, do the right things, and
say the right things. I went through the motions of the faith.
But over time, through various priests, friends, retreats, and
faith formation experiences, I came to realize that God doesn't
just love everyone in general, but that he loves *me*, Edward Sri,
personally. And that realization was life transforming. I used to
think I needed to go to Mass, say some prayers, be nice to other
people, and follow Church teachings just so that I could be a
good person, be a good Catholic, and get to heaven. Yet, God's
love cannot be earned. It can only be received. Only later did I

---

3   Paul Murray, *I Loved Jesus in the Night: Teresa of Calcutta; A Secret Revealed* (Brewster,
MA: Paraclete, 2008), 73.

come to see how there's much more to all those beliefs, rituals, and moral practices—how they are ultimately all about God's love for me and my relationship with him.

On a catechism quiz, if I were asked, "True or false: God loves you," I certainly would have answered, "True." But I can't say I was living from that truth deep in my heart day to day until I encountered God's love for me *personally*, realizing not merely that he loves me along with everyone one else but that he loves me specifically—with all my faults, weaknesses, hurts, and sins—and is awaiting my response. He is thirsting for me. He is longing for my soul. He is yearning for my time, my attention, my heart.

Mother Teresa, the saints, and countless ordinary Christian disciples throughout the ages have come to a point of marveling over this amazing personal love God has for them. What about you? Have you ever stopped to consider how much the all-powerful, all-knowing God of the universe— the God who doesn't need anything and who is "infinitely perfect and blessed in himself"—loves you, specifically you, personally? He brought you into existence for a reason, for a purpose. He wants to share his love with you. He is longing for you to spend time with him, to follow him, to entrust your life to him. How will you respond?

Image and Likeness

Let's next consider how Genesis also reveals something remarkable about man and woman, something that sets them apart from everything else in all creation. Nothing else in the universe receives this divine declaration—not the birds or the fish, the mountains or the seas, the animals or the stars. Only man and woman are revealed to be made in God's *image and likeness* (see Gen 1:26).

What does this mean? Three things ...

First, being created in God's image and likeness points to how *we are made to know and to love.* On a basic level, being made in God's image and likeness points to how we as human persons are made for relationship with God. God, who is all-knowing, gives us a share in his knowing power (the intellect). And God, who also is all-loving, gives us a share in his ability to choose and to love (the will). Unlike anything else in all creation, we are made to know and to love. We are made for friendship. We are made, ultimately, to know and love God himself.

Second, being made in God's image and likeness points to how *we are God's children.* It reveals the unique relationship God calls us to. In the Bible, the expression "image and likeness" has a specific meaning. It describes not just any kind of relationship, but one of the most profound relationships that exists: that between a father and a child. The next time this expression is used in the Bible, this point is made clear. It describes the relationship between Adam and his son Seth. Adam has a child named Seth, and Seth is said to be "in [Adam's] own likeness, after his image" (5:3). In Scripture, therefore, "image and likeness" points to sonship. (We might use a similar expression in our culture today to describe a son who looks like his father: "He's the spitting image of his dad!"). So, if man and woman are made in the image and likeness of God, that tells us something very important about who we are: we are God's children. Unlike anything else in all of creation, we are made for a personal relationship with God as his sons and daughters.

This stands in stark contrast to the stories other ancient cultures told about the origins of mankind. In many of those stories, men and women were merely the result of gods fighting, gods having sexual relations, or deities creating human beings merely to be served or entertained by them—not part of a larger noble plan, and certainly not rooted in love.

This Genesis account of Creation also stands in stark contrast to the empty modern, secular presupposition that there is no intrinsic meaning or purpose to life—that we are just randomly here. This view claims that there is no purpose to our existence and that it doesn't matter what we do with our lives. We are not created by God for a grand purpose. We are left on our own to give our lives meaning. But the early chapters of Genesis remind us that our lives are part of a much larger story: the story of God's love. You are not here by chance. You are not here without a purpose. You are not here alone. God created you out of love, and he created you for love. He created you to share in his life, share in his love, and be united in relationship with him for all eternity.

Third, the expression "image and likeness" tells us something important about God: *God is our loving Father.* If we are his children, then God is not just a creator, an all-powerful master, the ruler of the universe. Nor is he merely a supreme being, a vague, impersonal spiritual force, like in Star Wars. Nor is he a spectator God who created the universe but then just sits back and watches, uninvolved in our lives. No. The first chapter of the Bible reveals the remarkable truth that God is a personal God; indeed, he is a loving Father, who created us for a close relationship with him as his children.

I Thirst

To help interiorize the profound relationship with God that we are made for, prayerfully reflect on the following meditation based on the spiritual teachings of Mother Teresa. The prayer was written by Father Joseph Langford, a Missionary of Charity priest who worked closely with Mother Teresa. The meditation invites us to ponder the reality of God's love for us: a love that is at the heart of his creating us, holding us in existence, delighting in us, and thirsting for our response. Imagine Jesus speaking the following words to you personally:

> I stand at the door of your heart, day and night. Even when you are not listening, even when you doubt it could be me, I am there. I await even the smallest sign of your response, even the slightest hint of invitation that will allow me to enter.
>
> I want you to know that whenever you invite me, I come. Always, without fail....
>
> I know what is in your heart. I know your loneliness and all your hurts: the rejections, the judgments, the humiliations. I carried it all before you. And I carried it all for you so you might share my strength and victory. I know especially your need for love, how you thirst to be accepted and appreciated, loved and cherished. But how often you have thirsted in vain seeking that love outside of me—I who am its Source—striving to fill that emptiness inside you with passing pleasures....
>
> Do you thirst to be appreciated and cherished? I cherish you more than you can imagine, to the point of leaving heaven for you, and of dying on the cross to make you one with me.
>
> *I THIRST FOR YOU....* Yes, that is the only way to even begin to describe my love for you: I thirst to love you and to be loved by you—that is how precious you are to me.
>
> If you feel unimportant in the eyes of the world, that matters not at all. For me, there is no one more important in the entire world than you....
>
> All your life I have been looking for your love—I have never stopped seeking to love you and to be loved by you. You have tried many other things in your search for happiness.

Why not try opening your heart to me, right now, more than you have ever done before? ... I stand at the door of your heart and knock. Open to me, for I thirst for you.[4]

Reflection Questions:

1. What struck you most from the "I Thirst" meditation?
2. How do the themes from the meditation change the way you view God?
3. How do you think God is inviting you to respond to his thirst for your love?

---

4 Joseph Langford, *Mother Teresa's Secret Fire: The Encounter That Changed St. Teresa of Calcutta's Life and How It Can Transform Your Own* (Huntington, IN: Our Sunday Visitor, 2008), 297–301.

Chapter 4

Part 2: Rebellion—
Fallen Angels, Fallen Humanity

When the twentieth-century Catholic writer G. K. Chesterton was asked, "What's wrong with the world?" he gave a most unexpected answer.

He could have talked about war, wicked leaders, corporate greed, or incompetent governments. He could have discussed poverty, immorality, sexual sin, or attacks on human life. Instead, when asked, "What's wrong with the world?" he gave a simple, yet profound two-word answer: "I am."

Whatever one may believe about religion, no one can deny that there are many problems and a whole lot of suffering in this world. And this is not just an abstract, philosophical observation. It's something very personal to all of us. None of us can escape our own share in suffering. We all are going to have moments and seasons of loneliness, hurt, disappointment, frustration, and sorrow. Some of us will experience the pains in life more intensely. Others will endure much longer periods of anguish. And all of us are going to experience the ultimate form of suffering: death.

But why do we experience suffering? The modern, secular view of the world might lead us to believe that the root of all our problems is not us, but something outside us. We might tell ourselves, *I have good desires. I want to live a happy life. It's other people who have hurt me, frustrated my plans, or kept me from fulfilling my desires. Maybe it's my parents, my peers, my boss, my community. Or perhaps it's the government, society, the economic system, the media. Or maybe it's a certain nation, race, religion, group of people, political party, or ideology. Yes, there are many problems in the world. And I have many personal frustrations and sufferings. If we could just fix certain other people, then we could make the world a better place and I could finally be happy.*

Chesterton, however, invites us to look elsewhere for the root of our sufferings: our own hearts. This is not to say there are not injustices in the world that need to be addressed—real evils that impact the world as a whole and our individual lives. But the main source of these evils is not "out there" in the world but deep within human souls. It is injustice and evil in the human heart that brings about the injustices and evils in the world. And if we take an honest look, we will admit that we have some of those injustices and evils in our own hearts.

Indeed, we will find a wound in our souls, a tendency to seek what is not good. That's what even the great apostle Saint Paul once admitted. When he examined his life, he noticed a deep wound in his soul, a mysterious inability to do what he knew he should and an inclination pulling in the opposite direction, leading him to do things he didn't want to do: "I do not understand my own actions. For I do not do what I want, but I do the very thing I hate.... For I do not do the good I want, but the evil I do not want is what I do. Now if I do what I do not want, it is no longer I that do it, but sin which dwells within me" (Rom 7:15, 19–20).

Can you relate? Do you have areas in your life where you want to be better—to be kinder, more generous, more disciplined, more patient, more forgiving, more sacrificial, living in service to God and others and not just yourself? Do you have areas where you've even tried to improve but you still struggle? No matter how hard you try to be better, do you sometimes still fall into selfishness, pride, envy, or lust? If you do not have any of these struggles and have already reached perfection, please let me know. That means you should be made a canonized saint!

But if we're honest, we all have areas where we fall short. We all have many moments when Saint Paul's words resonate with us: "I do not do what I want", and "I do the very thing I hate." We tell ourselves we're not going to procrastinate, hold a grudge, complain, compare ourselves to others, be afraid, get anxious, lose our tempers, eat too much, or give in to a lustful glance … and then later we find ourselves doing the very thing we told ourselves we did not want to do. It is this fundamental, universal experience of human weakness that multiplies suffering and evil in this world.

But why do we each have this tendency to struggle, this inability to do what we know we should? What is this wound in the human heart? Where does it come from? Many Christians might answer, "Original Sin." And that would be a very good, correct response. But there is something even deeper we must consider, something sinister at work behind this reality that Christians call "Original Sin". Indeed, there's a darker power that originally led us into sin and now has a hold on us, dividing us from God and from one another and keeping us from experiencing true freedom, true happiness, and fullness of life.

Darkness and the Shining One

Some of the most significant things in life are the things we cannot see.

Before he created the physical universe, God created the invisible, spiritual realm, which the Bible calls "the heavens" (Gen 1:1). This refers to the angels—the spectacular beings that are more magnificent than the tallest mountain peak, the depth of the ocean, or the billions of stars in the Milky Way galaxy. God created the angels to reflect his own life, giving them intelligent minds and free will to know and to love. Unlike us, however, angels do not have bodies, so they are beyond the physical realm. As pure spirits, they cannot be seen. Though they interact in our world all the time, our senses are not able to detect their presence.

Why did God create the angels? To know and love him and to serve him, especially in caring for the second part of creation that God would bring about next: the physical universe, which includes us human beings.

One angel, however, stood out from all the others. His name was "light bearer" or "shining one", indicating how gloriously gifted he must have been. God endowed this angel with more of his strength, power, and glory than he did all the others. How splendid it must have been to look upon this angel who radiated God's glory the most!

Along with all the other angels, the "shining one" was put to a test. God did not force the angels to serve him. He gave them freedom to make a choice. So, before they could see God face-to-face, they had to decide whether they would serve God. A great multitude of the angels saw the sheer goodness of God and responded to this test in love, choosing to serve and worship God. The "light bearer", however, made the opposite choice. He pridefully saw his magnificence as his own, not as a gift from God. Captivated by his own beauty, intelligence, and power, he foolishly chose to declare independence from his Creator. With a blind "false sense of self-sufficiency", this angel sought to build his own kingdom instead of serving God's.[1] And he convinced many other angels to join his rebellion.

---

[1]   John Paul II, General Audience, July 23, 1986, in *A Catechesis on the Creed*, vol. 1, *God, Father and Creator* (Boston: Pauline Books & Media, 1996), 294–96.

Let's ponder that for a moment. This angel actually thought he could be independent from his Creator! And he seduced many other angels into this lie. This shows how influential the "light bearer" must have been! Today, this angel is known as Lucifer, for Lucifer means "light bearer". He goes by other names as well: the devil (meaning "divider, scatterer"), Satan (meaning "the accuser"), and "the ruler of this world". He and the other angels who set themselves against God worked together to disrupt God's plan in any way they could. They knew they could not destroy God himself, so they set their eyes on the pinnacle of God's creation: man and woman. Lucifer hoped to use his cunning power to seduce them to join his rebellion as well, bringing them under his reign of sin and death.

The Four Harmonies

We saw in the previous chapter how God made man and woman as the summit of his creation, creating them in his image and likeness with the powers to know and to love so that they could live in relationship with him. Let's take a closer look now at this gift of creation and consider what can be called "the four harmonies" that God originally gave man and woman.

First, man and woman each originally lived in *harmony with God*. They were filled with God's life and lived in friendship with him.

Second, flowing from that life of God within them, man and woman experienced *harmony within their own souls*. They had an internal equilibrium, with their mind, will, and passions all working well together and directed toward what is good and true.

As a result of this inner harmony, man and woman experienced two other harmonies: *harmony in their relationship with each other* and *harmony with all creation*, not being subject to illness, decay, or fear of death. They were meant to live forever.

But Lucifer and the other rebellious angels hated these four great blessings in Adam and Eve. Seeing the joy, goodness, and love that our first parents shared with God filled the devil and the other fallen angels with envy and anger. Though they had been cast out of heaven, they could still invade the visible realm and oppose God there. So, they sought to destroy the love and unity that God gave to man and woman.

Back to the Garden

To understand what happened next, we need to look at a famous story from the Bible that you might have heard before, perhaps from your childhood. But I invite you to read this story with new eyes—more mature eyes—as an adult, not a child, in order to see what's really there. It's a story filled with much intricacy, symbolism, and literary art that, while not meant to be taken in a literalistic way, nevertheless gives us an important window into what really happened at the beginning of the human family. It's the story of Adam and Eve.

First, carefully ponder what the Bible says about the one prohibition God gave Adam and Eve in the Garden of Eden: "You may freely eat of every tree of the garden; but of the tree of the knowledge of good and evil you shall not eat, for in the day that you eat of it you shall die" (Gen 2:16–17).

According to these verses, did God give this command in order to restrict Adam and Eve? To control them? No. The Bible makes clear that God gave them a vast freedom to eat "freely" from "every tree of the garden". There's only one tree they are warned not to eat from.

And why did God tell them not to eat from this tree? Because God did not want them to get hurt: "For in the day that you eat of it you shall die." Here, we see that God did not give this command as a random rule to restrict Adam and Eve. Rather, God loves his children and wanted to protect them from some mysterious danger symbolized by this tree.[2] God's law flows from his love. This rule flows from his relationship with man and woman.

The Deceiver

The devil is cunning. His attack on the man and woman was not a direct one; he took a subtler and more sinister approach.

Consider the devil's initial move. He didn't say, "Hi, do you want to join my rebellion against God today?" Nor did he try to convince them to become atheists, to lie, to steal, or to murder. He was not primarily interested in getting Adam and Eve merely to break a rule. He wanted to go after the heart of their *relationship* with God by stirring up doubt: Is God really a loving Father? Does this God really love you and want to live in friendship with you? Is God really trustworthy? The devil's first words were "Did God say, 'You shall not eat of any tree of the garden'?" (Gen 3:1).

There's a lot happening in this opening line. First, the devil referred to the Lord as "God" (*Elohim* in Hebrew). That's the title used in Genesis 1 to describe God as the Creator. But in Genesis 2–3, this Creator God is revealed to be "Lord God" (*Yahweh Elohim*)—a name that is used elsewhere in the Bible to describe God's closeness with his people, his covenant

---

2   "The 'tree of the knowledge of good and evil' symbolically evokes the insurmountable limits that man, being a creature, must fully recognize and respect with trust. Man is dependent on his Creator and subject to the laws of creation and to the moral norms that govern the use of freedom" (*CCC* 396, quoting Gen 2:17). Eating of the tree, therefore, would point to man's rebellion against these limitations and to his desire to be like God himself. "Seduced by the devil, he wanted to 'be like God' but 'without God, before God, and not in accordance with God' " (*CCC* 398).

friendship with them. For example, Genesis 2 describes the
"Lord God" creating Adam and breathing life into him, putting him in the beautiful garden, walking closely with him
in the garden, allowing him to name the animals, and creating the woman from his side. In other words, the "Lord
God" is not just a supreme power and Creator of the vast universe—he is also a loving, personal God, involved in Adam
and Eve's lives, living in close friendship with them, and providing for them.

But the devil hates all this. He himself rejected the goodness and love of God, and he wanted the man and woman
to do the same. So he painted a picture not of a loving God
but of a distant deity who was interested only in limiting and
controlling them. He wanted to plant a seed of doubt about
God in their minds. It's as if the devil said, *Did that remote
Creator God say to you, 'You shall not eat of any of the trees of the
garden'? . . . Why is he restricting you?* Though God gave them
tremendous freedom, saying, "You may *freely* eat of *every* tree
of the garden" (2:16, emphasis added), the devil focused on
just the one tree God warned them about.

When the woman responded to the devil, she did not focus
on the vast freedom God gave them to eat from every other
tree in the garden. She instead zoomed in on the one tree the
devil wanted her to zoom in on, saying that if they ate of the
tree "in the midst of the garden", they would die (3:2–3).[3]

The devil had succeeded in his first move. He drew her
attention to the restriction and caused her to become suspi-
cious about God. We can imagine her wondering, *Why did
God say we would die if we ate from this tree?* The devil then
leaned in for his decisive strike. He said to her, "You will

---

3   In addition, the woman exaggerated the restriction regarding the tree of the knowledge of
good and evil, saying, "Neither shall [we] touch it" (3:3). This indicates how she was starting
to buy in to the devil's picture of God as restrictive.

not die. For God knows that when you eat of it your eyes will be opened, and you will be like God, knowing good and evil" (3:4).

Take a moment to realize what the devil was really doing here. First, when he said, "You will not die", he was not merely making a claim that they would still be alive if they ate from the tree. It's much worse than that. He was calling God a liar! According to the devil, the tree was *not* harmful, as God said it was. It's as if the devil was saying, "God told you that you would die if you ate from this tree?... No! That's not true! You will not die. God is not trustworthy. He has been lying to you."

Second, the devil went on to offer a motive for why God was lying to them: because "you will be like God." In other words, the devil was telling Adam and Eve that the only reason God gave this command was that he wanted to control them. He wanted to suppress them. God told them it was harmful because he feared that if they ate from the tree, they would become like him.

This was the devil's strategy. He was not just trying to get Adam and Eve to break a rule. He was ultimately trying to get them to break a *relationship*. He wanted to separate the law of God from the love of God and convince man and woman to view this command as an oppressive restriction—a restriction that's keeping man and woman in their place and preventing them from discovering true fulfillment and becoming as great as they could be.

Here, we can begin to see how the devil's temptation was much more intense than the typical children's book portrayal of a snake trying to get a woman to eat an apple. There was so much more happening! The devil was trying to get Adam and Eve to doubt God's goodness and love. As the *Catechism* explains, "Man, tempted by the devil, let his trust in his Creator die in his heart and, abusing his freedom, disobeyed God's command. This is what man's first sin consisted of. All subsequent sin would be disobedience toward God and lack of trust in his goodness" (*CCC* 397).[4]

Abolishing Fatherhood

Step back for a moment and feel the weight of all that is happening in these events at the beginning of time. God didn't have to create us. He is perfect and glorious in himself. Yet he freely chose to bring us into existence in order to share his life and love with us. He is a loving Father, and he made us for relationship with him as his children.

With this background in mind, we can see how the first sin isn't just about breaking a commandment from God and failing to pass a test. Rather, the first sin goes so much deeper. It broke that relationship with God, as man and woman didn't trust his love and goodness toward them. Saint John Paul II put it this way: "Original sin is not only the violation of a positive command of God but also, and above all, a violation of *the will of God as expressed in that command. Original sin attempts, then, to abolish fatherhood,* destroying its rays which permeate the created world, placing in doubt the truth about God who is Love."[5]

Indeed, Adam and Eve fell for the devil's lie that God was jealous of them, that God was keeping them from a wonderful life, and that all they had to do was reject their reliance on God and they could find true fulfillment and become great like God himself. So, they declared their independence from

---

4   Cf. Gen 3:1–11; Rom 5:19.
5   John Paul II, *Crossing the Threshold of Hope* (New York: Alfred A. Knopf, 1994), 228.

God, and ate from the tree—then everything was changed in an instant.

Everything Turned Upside Down

As a result of the first sin, everything in the universe was immediately turned upside down. The devil convinced man and woman to join his rebellion against the Creator, and a dramatic rupture ensued. Now "the whole world is in the power of the Evil One" (1 Jn 5:19), and man and woman right away lost the four beautiful harmonies in which they were created.

First and foremost, *they lost their harmony with God*, their sharing in his life. In breaking God's command, man and woman chose to declare their independence from God. As a result, they lost that supernatural life of God dwelling within them and no longer were living in friendship with him.

And this rupture in our relationship with God is the root of all the problems we face on earth today. We see this in the other three harmonies we lost. *We lost the inner harmony within our souls*. Our minds became clouded and more easily stray into falsehood; our wills are weakened, and it's harder for us to choose what is good. Our emotions and bodily desires often take over, and we are not easily able to rule our souls by the light of truth. We notice a tendency toward selfishness and resonate with the experience of Saint Paul: "I do not do what I want", and "I do the very thing I hate."

We also *lost the harmony we had with one another*. With this tendency toward sin, our relationships are now often tainted by self-centeredness, division, hurt, and the use of one another. And we *lost the original harmony with all creation*. We will not live here forever. Our bodies will be subject to suffering, disease, decay, and death.

The loss of the four harmonies was passed on from our first parents to us today. This is the reality Christians call Original Sin.[6]

But there is another aspect of this tragedy that is not often realized. When we are living apart from God, it's not as if we are just on our own, separated from our Creator. When man and woman declared their independence from God, it's not as if they simply turned away from God's kingdom and were living in a neutral land. Rather, they put themselves— and the human family—into enemy territory. After the Fall, the human family is now besieged by the reign of the enemy.

As the *Catechism* explains, "The devil has acquired a certain dominion over man.... Original sin entails 'captivity under the power of him who thenceforth had the power of death, that is, the devil'" (*CCC* 407).[7] Indeed, through man and woman's cooperation with the devil, Lucifer has become "the ruler of this world" (Jn 12:31), and we all suffer the consequences: "All men ... are under the power of sin" (Rom 3:9). And without God to rescue us, we would be trapped in sin and death and eternally separated from the love of God.

Indeed, the first sin is the most radical rupture ever to have taken place in the universe. And though the modern world doesn't like to talk about it, sin's consequences are utterly devastating. As Saint Catherine of Siena described, there is now an infinite chasm between the human family and God. And there is nothing we can do on our own to bridge this chasm.

---

6   But here we must be clear. Original Sin is not the passing on of the personal sin of Adam and Eve, as if we are morally guilty for something they did long ago. Rather, Original Sin is a *lack* of something. It is the passing on of human nature without the gift of God's life. Since they lost that original holiness, man and woman did not have that supernatural life of God to pass on to the subsequent generations. Though we enter this world with natural, biological life, we are not born with the supernatural life of God in our souls. And without that original holiness that we were made for, we are severely handicapped. We are wounded. We no longer have the inner harmony in our souls, and we find ourselves often like Saint Paul: not doing the good we want to do and doing the evil we do not wish to do. We are fallen. We are wounded, struggling with inclinations toward sin and separated from God.

7   Quoting Council of Trent (1546): DS 1511; cf. Heb 2:14.

Without God's help, we would be eternally separated from God in hell, held captive and suffering under the power of the enemy forever.

A Promise and a Hope

God, however, does not abandon us. Even though man and woman "hid themselves from the presence of the LORD God" (Gen 3:8), which points to how they turned away from God in sin, God still sought them out. He had a plan to save them, and he announced this plan right away. Almost immediately after the Fall, God confronted the devil (symbolized by the serpent) and gave a prophetic foreshadowing of how he would free his people from sin, death, and the devil's reign. God punished the devil and foretold that, one day, the woman would have a descendant (her seed) who would defeat the devil: this future son would crush the head of the serpent (see 3:15; *CCC* 410).

But in this passage, God doesn't just talk about how he's going to save man. He also shows us. Consider how Genesis 3 describes Adam being *tested* in a *garden*—the Garden of Eden—and how he proved to be unfaithful to God, *not trusting God as his loving Father*. The passage goes on to describe how Adam will suffer various punishments. The ground that he will till will often bear only *thorns* and thistles. His labor will be difficult, causing *sweat* to run down his face, and he will experience *death*, with his body returning to the *ground* (see 3:18–19). All these details prefigure how God will solve the problem of sin.

For when God eventually sends the son of the woman—the one who is his own Son, Jesus Christ—this Son, at the climax of his mission, will endure the same trials Adam experienced. Jesus will be *tested* by the devil in a *garden*—the Garden of

Gethsemane—just like Adam was tested in a garden. In this garden, however, Jesus will prove to be faithful, where Adam was unfaithful. There, he will pray a prayer of surrender, *trusting God as his loving Father*. He will pray, "Not my will, but yours, be done" (Lk 22:42). While he prays, *sweat* like drops of blood will run down his face, recalling the curse of the sweat on Adam's brow. And the next day, Jesus will wear the crown of *thorns* on his head, recalling the curse of the thorns coming from the earth. Ultimately, Jesus will experience Adam's curse of *death* and return to the cursed *ground* when he's buried in the tomb. By taking on the curses of Adam, Jesus will bring them to completion, and from the darkness of the tomb in the cursed ground, the light of the world will shine when he rises from the dead on Easter.

Reflection Questions:

1. In what ways do you notice the effects of Original Sin in your life?

2. Regularly examining our consciences and telling God we are sorry for our sins is a key aspect of Christian prayer. But too often in prayer, we rush to our petitions and needs without taking time to confess our sins. When you pray, how often do you acknowledge your sins and express your sorrow to God for them? How often do you frequent the Sacrament of Reconciliation? How might God be inviting you to grow in this aspect of your spiritual life?

3. What particular weakness have you not been able to overcome on your own? Entrust that area of your life to God, and ask him for his grace to help you do what you cannot do by your own strength.

Chapter 5

Part 3: Reconciliation I— "Who Do You Say That I Am?"

The fact that God chose to rescue us is completely astounding. From a human perspective, it would have been understandable and fair if God chose to abandon man for having rejected him. But "God is love" (1 Jn 4:8). And he is so in love with us that even though we have turned away from him, he still seeks us out. He remains faithful to us, even when we are unfaithful to him. He still longs to be one with us. That's why he came to rescue us.

But what is even more astonishing is the *way* in which God came to save us. He didn't stay in heaven, snap his fingers, and use his power to liberate us from the hands of the enemy. Rather, he did the most unthinkable thing: the all-holy, all-powerful, infinite God chose to enter our finite, fallen world and actually become one of us. He took on our humanity in Jesus Christ. As Saint John's Gospel expresses it, "The Word became flesh and dwelt among us" (1:14).

Moreover, he didn't come in worldly glory, power, and might. There was no large army, no royal splendor, no grand entry onto the world's stage. Rather, the God of the universe— the King of kings and Lord of lords—came into this world as a child, born into poverty and humility and laid in a manger in the obscure town of Bethlehem, barely on the periphery of the great Roman Empire.

Still, the devil realized something significant was happening. He did not like the sight of angels rejoicing over the nearby fields and shepherds running in haste to reverence this newborn child lying in a manger. He wanted this child killed. So the devil stirred up Herod to massacre all the male children two years old and younger in the area. But God sent an angel to warn Joseph to flee with the child and his mother to Egypt.

The devil was alarmed again when the child showed up as a thirty-year-old to be baptized at the Jordan River. Satan noticed extraordinary supernatural events surrounding this baptism: the heavens opened, the Spirit fell on this child like a dove, and a voice from heaven declared, "This is my beloved Son, with whom I am well pleased" (Mt 3:17). So, after his baptism, when Jesus went out to the desert to pray and fast, the devil tried to tempt him like he tempted Adam and Eve. But Jesus outsmarted the devil and remained faithful to his Father. Lucifer, the "shining one"—the most magnificent and powerful of all the angels—realized he could not seduce this Son of God like he did Adam and Eve. Defeated in this opening battle, the devil regrouped to consider his next move in the larger war. Luke's Gospel tells us that the devil departed from Jesus "until an opportune time" (4:13).

What was the devil so worried about? What did he sense in Jesus that made him so alarmed? God had sent teachers, messengers, and prophets before. How was Jesus different?

More Than a Teacher

Christianity is unique among all the other major religions of the world in that it is not primarily an idea, a set of moral and spiritual principles, or a way of life. At the heart of Christianity is a person: Jesus Christ, the divine Son of God who became man and dwelt among us. Jesus is different from other religious leaders like Buddha or Muhammad, who claimed to be a spiritual teacher, a prophet, or a messenger from God— someone pointing the way to God or inner peace. Jesus claimed to be so much more than that. He didn't just offer a spiritual way, a religious truth, or a fulfilled life. He said, "*I am* the way, and the truth, and the life" (Jn 14:6, emphasis added). He made himself the central issue. In other words, he didn't simply tell people to believe in God in order to be saved. Jesus proclaimed that "whoever believes in *him* may have eternal life" (3:15, emphasis added).

Jesus wasn't just a teacher, instructing people *about* God. He claimed to be God himself. We see this in many ways.

First, Jesus forgave people's sins, which is something only God can do. I might forgive my neighbor for doing something that hurt me personally. But I don't have the power to forgive all the sins he has ever committed against God throughout his life. That's something only God can do. Yet it was this kind of comprehensive forgiveness that Jesus offered people throughout his ministry—a forgiveness of *all* their sins. And this is why the Jewish leaders were so upset when Jesus did this. For example, when he forgave the sins of a paralyzed man, the Pharisees accused Jesus of blasphemy, saying, "Who can forgive sins but God only?" (Lk 5:21). They understood what Jesus was doing. They knew Jesus was claiming to do what only God can do, and they did not like it.

We see this even more in Jesus' words. In the Sermon on the Mount, Jesus referred to the Jewish Old Testament Law in a way that asserted an authority no Jewish teacher had dared to assert before. The Jews believed that the Law (the Torah) was given by God. Several times in the Sermon on the Mount (see Mt 5:21–48), Jesus said, "You have heard that it was said ..." and then he quoted or alluded to the Law—something other Jewish rabbis commonly did. But what Jesus said next would have been completely shocking. After quoting from the Law of God, he said, "But I say to you ..."

Think about what that would mean. Imagine if a colleague in your workplace said, "You heard the CEO of the company say ... But *I* say to you ..." Such a statement would be surprising coming from an ordinary coworker. In speaking this way, your colleague would be putting his authority on par with the CEO!

Now consider how much more shocking Jesus' words would have been in the first-century Jewish context. Jesus quoted from the Law that came from God himself and then said, "But I say to you ..." Such a statement would be astonishing coming from a mere human being. In speaking like this, however, Jesus was claiming to be no ordinary human teacher. He was assuming a divine authority, equal to the heavenly Father's. This is why the crowds were so astonished at Jesus' teachings—because he taught with an authority they had never encountered before. He taught with the authority of God.

Consider two other provocative statements Jesus made about his identity. In Jerusalem, Jesus said to the crowds, "I and the Father are one" (Jn 10:30). This is not the way an ordinary Jew would ever speak about his relationship with God. In talking like this, Jesus was claiming to be on par with God himself. That's why the people listening to Jesus didn't like it. They accused him of blasphemy and picked up stones to kill him, saying, "You, being a man, make yourself God" (10:33).

On another occasion, Jesus took the Jewish divine name that God revealed to Moses—Yahweh, or "I AM" (Ex 3:14), and applied it to himself. He said, "Before Abraham was, I am" (Jn 8:58). This revealed name of God was considered so holy that no ancient Jew would even speak it. For Jesus to allude to the holy, divine name and then apply it to himself would have been utterly astonishing. The Jews were horrified. Once again, they viewed this as blasphemy and picked up stones to put him to death (see 8:59).

"Who Do You Say That I Am?"

It's clear that Jesus said and did things that only God would say and do. So, how do we respond to someone who claims to have the authority of God himself? By speaking and acting in the Person of God, Jesus challenges us to make a choice about him. The question he posed to his apostles some two thousand years ago, he continues to ask us today: "Who do you say that I am?" (Mt 16:15).

And this is a very personal question. Is Jesus just a good teacher? One religious option, one spiritual guide among many? Or is Jesus vastly different from all the others? Is he who he claimed to be? Is he truly Lord?

Some people might prefer to avoid this question. If Jesus is who he said he is—if he really is God—then that means I have to follow him. If he really is God, then what he teaches is true—and not just for some people but for everyone, including me. So, if Jesus is God, I need to do what he says. If he really is Lord, I might have to start making changes in how I live. I will have to start living according to God's plan for my life, not my own. If Jesus is God, then I will need to embrace, at the core of my being, the fundamental truth that God once spoke to Saint Catherine of Siena: "I'm God; you're not."

But what if I don't want to change and give up doing whatever I want? If, in the end, I want to continue making up my own morality, my own values, and my own truth instead of surrendering to what Jesus teaches and asks of me—then it's easier to say Jesus is just a good man, a wise teacher, one of the many spiritual leaders the world has to offer. If I want, I can admire this kind of Jesus, be inspired by him, and apply some of his wisdom to my life. But I can also choose to set aside the parts of Jesus' teachings that don't match up with my lifestyle and that challenge me to change.

The "just a good teacher" Jesus is easy to accept. That kind of Jesus I can control. I can have that Jesus be a part of my life, but on my terms. I can keep a sense of Jesus in my life without having to follow him completely. I can pick and choose which parts of Jesus' teaching I want to fit into my life while conveniently setting aside other parts. But when I do that, I merely end up constructing a God who likes what I like, loves what I love, approves of what I approve of, and condemns what I condemn. And at that point, I will have created God in my image, rather than allowing my life to be conformed to who he really is.

Lord, Liar, or Lunatic?

But the real Jesus won't let us get away with that. The real Jesus challenges us to make a choice about him. The real Jesus is very different from Buddha, Muhammad, and other leaders of the world's major religions in this most significant way: *Jesus claimed to be God.* So, as C. S. Lewis once explained, Jesus is either who he said he is—Lord of the universe—or he is a liar or a lunatic. The one thing we can't say about Jesus is that he's "just a good man".

Let's consider the three logical options before us: Jesus is either a liar, a lunatic, or Lord.

> *Option 1—Liar:* Jesus knew he was not God but claimed to be, deceptively tricking people into thinking he was God. In this case, he would have been far from a good man. He would have been a wicked liar, who deceived people.
>
> *Option 2—Lunatic:* Jesus sincerely thought he was God but wasn't. He was deluded, a crazy person, far from a good, wise spiritual teacher.
>
> *Option 3—Lord:* Jesus is who he claimed to be. He is God.

In neither the first nor the second scenario would we say Jesus is a good man we should follow, a good teacher we should learn from. After all, someone who wickedly deceives millions of people into thinking he's God is not a good man but an evil one. And if your colleague came into the office on Monday morning telling everyone he suddenly realized he was God, you would conclude he has gone a bit crazy. You might feel sorry for him. But you wouldn't say he is a good teacher, a trusted guide, someone we should follow. You'd say he was a lunatic.

The one thing we can't logically conclude is that Jesus is "just a good man". Jesus made unique claims about his divine authority that challenge us to make a choice about him. We must decide: Is Jesus who he said he is—Lord? Or is he a liar or a lunatic? If he is a liar, we must oppose him and help others not be deceived by his lies. If he is a lunatic, we can have compassion for him, but we must help people not be fooled into following a crazy person. But if Jesus is who he said he is—if Jesus is Lord—then that has massive consequences for our lives. If Jesus is truly Lord, then we must entrust every aspect of our lives to him and follow him.

Imagine Jesus looking you in the eye and asking, "Who do *you* say that I am?" How would you respond?

Reflection Questions:

1. How is Jesus different from every other religious leader, teacher, or spiritual guide?
2. What does the fact that God became one of us tell us about God? What do you appreciate most about this mystery of God becoming man?
3. Picture Jesus asking you personally the same question he asked the apostles: "Who do you say that I am?" How would you respond?

Chapter 6

Part 3: Reconciliation II— The Cross

Imagine you were crossing a street with a friend and didn't see a speeding car that was about to hit you. Your friend noticed and pushed you out of the way, stepping in front of the car so you wouldn't get hit. But in the process your friend died. What would you think about your friend? Your friend just died ... *for you.*

Jesus, of course, is like that friend. "Greater love has no man than this, that a man lay down his life for his friends" (Jn 15:13).

But we Christians often take the Cross for granted. We might acknowledge that Jesus died for our sins like we acknowledge other facts about our Catholic faith: There are ten commandments. There are seven sacraments. Jesus was born in Bethlehem. The pope lives in Rome. Jesus died for our sins.

But Jesus' death on Calvary is not just one of many facts about the Christian faith. It is at the very center. The Cross is the fullest revelation of God's love for us. When we look at the Cross, we see Love himself most fully. Indeed, we see that love is not an idea, a feeling, a passion. Love is a Person—a Person who died for you. How will you respond?

The Cross: A Successful Rescue Mission?

In the previous chapter, we saw how, after Jesus resisted the three temptations in the desert, the devil retreated. Satan lost the first battle against Christ. But he was biding his time, plotting his next move. As Luke's Gospel explains, the devil "departed from him until an opportune time" (4:13).

That opportune time came after Jesus arrived in Jerusalem for Passover, on what today is known as Palm Sunday. After the devil saw the people welcoming Jesus as their king, waving palm branches and shouting out, "Hosanna to the Son of David!" (Mt 21:9), he began to mount his final attack. The devil stirred two rival groups of Jewish leaders who normally didn't like to work together—the chief priests and the Pharisees—to conspire against Jesus and condemn him to death. And then he induced these two groups to work with their oppressors, the Romans, to have Jesus crucified. The Bible even describes how Satan entered one of Jesus' own disciples, Judas, to entice him to betray Jesus. He then sifted the other disciples like wheat, as all but one abandoned Jesus when the devil's "power of darkness" came upon them in the Garden of Gethsemane (Lk 22:53). From a human perspective, we see Judas, Caiaphas, Pontius Pilate, and Roman soldiers bringing Jesus to his death. But the Scriptures reveal the darker power at work that day. And as a result, Jesus was condemned by the Jewish leaders, handed over to the Romans, and crucified. Jesus, the Son of God, was killed on Good Friday and buried in a tomb.

But here we might ask, "How is this a successful rescue mission? I thought Jesus was supposed to rescue us from the devil! Instead, he found *himself* captured, humiliated, and killed, suffering the most torturous death known in ancient times: Roman crucifixion. How does this possibly solve the problem of mankind's sin?"

These are fair questions. From a human perspective, Jesus on the cross does not look like a victorious king, triumphing over the enemy. From a human perspective, he looks like a tragic failure. So, even though Christians often say, "Jesus died for my sins," *what does that really mean*? How does the death of an innocent man rescue us from sin, death, and the devil?

The Triumph of the Cross

According to some Christians, the main point of the Cross is that Jesus volunteered to take on our punishment. We sinned against God. We deserve to be punished. God could have poured his wrath upon us. But instead, God lovingly sent his only beloved Son, Jesus, to die for us. Jesus, the innocent one, freely chose to receive the punishment that we deserve so that we can be saved. From this perspective, this is the main reason Jesus died for our sins.

But this is not a Catholic view of the Cross. Think about it: a God who pours out punishment on an innocent person would not be a God of mercy or justice. It is not just to punish the innocent, nor is it merciful. So there must be more to Jesus' death on Calvary than this. Jesus' death on the cross saves us not because some innocent person received the punishment that a guilty party deserved, thereby fulfilling justice somehow. Such a view paints a picture of God the Father as a deity with thousands of years of pent-up anger that is finally unleashed on his innocent Son, who stepped in to take our punishment.

In the Catholic view of the Cross, the focus is more on love than on punishment. As the *Catechism* explains, "It is love 'to the end' that confers on Christ's sacrifice its value as redemption and reparation, as atonement and satisfaction"

(*CCC* 616).[1] Many Christians—and unfortunately, even many Catholics—don't understand the Cross correctly. How about you? Would you be able to explain the Cross clearly to a friend or to your child in a truly Catholic way? It's essential we get this central aspect of Christianity right.

Let's now take a closer look at a Catholic view on how the Cross works—how it brings about our salvation.

A Gift of Love

If we hurt someone we love, we want to do something to repair the relationship. We need to perform some act of love to make amends, to make up for our lack of love. If, for example, I say something that hurts my wife, I tell her I'm sorry. If it's a deeper hurt, I might hold her hand or put my arm around her as a gesture of my love for her. I desire to offer a tangible expression of love to make up for my lack of love. And if it's an even more serious hurt, I might get her flowers, perform some act of service, or buy her a box of her favorite chocolates! I desire to perform a meaningful act of love to make up for my lack of love. And the greatness of that act of love should correspond to the level of hurt inflicted on the relationship.

The same is true with God. When we sin, we withhold the love that we owe to God, who so generously loves us. So we should offer an act of love that corresponds to the gravity of our sin. But the gravity of our sin is infinite. Indeed, when we sin against our infinitely good, holy, and glorious God, we need to offer not just any expression of love but, because of who God is, an *infinite* gift of love to restore our relationship with him.

But no human being can do that. Not even the holiest person could do that. We are finite creatures. No mere human

---

1   Quoting Jn 13:1.

being is capable of offering an *infinite* gift of love that would atone for the sins of all mankind. Only an infinite God could do that.[2]

So, here's the great dilemma: to reconcile with God—to make amends and atone for his sin—man *should* offer God an infinite gift of love. But man *can't* do that. Only an infinite God can do that. That's why a God-man is necessary. Only someone who is truly divine and truly human could solve the problem of mankind's sin. And that's why God became man in Jesus Christ. Jesus is the God-man.

First, Jesus is *fully human*. God loved us so much that he took on our humanity in Jesus Christ. As one of us, Jesus can represent us. He can offer a gift of love on behalf of the human family.

Second, Jesus is also *fully divine*. As God, his act of love takes on infinite value.

Therefore, on the cross, Jesus Christ, who is fully God and fully man, can represent the entire human family, offering himself as the infinite gift of total, self-giving love on our behalf. Love is stronger than death, and the perfect gift of love offered for us on Calvary restores us to right relationship with God, frees us from death, and liberates us from the enemy.

Now we can appreciate why the *Catechism* says "it is love 'to the end'" that gives the Cross its redemptive value (*CCC* 616).[3] It's not the amount of blood that was shed or bones that were broken or tears that dripped down his cheek. Indeed, as Saint Bernard of Clairvaux is often quoted as saying, "The smallest drop of Christ's blood would have been enough to redeem all mankind."[4] For, even in that tiniest drop of Christ's blood, God's infinite love is being offered. It is Jesus' self-giving love—his total, perfect, beautiful love

---

2 St. Anselm asked, since we owe God our entire lives already—all our love, service, obedience—what could we possibly give him that we don't owe him already?

3 Quoting Jn 13:1.

4 Thomas Aquinas, *Questionis Quodlibertales* II. Q. I. a. 2.

expressed through his suffering on the cross—that gives the Cross its saving power. Saint Catherine of Siena put it this way: the nails would not have held him to the cross if love had not held him there first.[5]

The Father's Love

But in what sense does Jesus suffer for our sins?

Imagine a father and son hiking in the mountains alongside a river. The father warns the son not to go too close to the river since it has a powerful current and he could be swept away by the cold rushing waters with many dangerous twists and turns, branches, and large rocks. But the child does not heed his father's warning. He draws near to the river and falls in. The current sweeps the child away.

What will the father do? He doesn't hesitate. Out of love for his son, he immediately jumps in to save him. But in the process, the father experiences all the pains his son does—the ice-cold water, the river carrying him against his will, his choking from inhaling water, his body bleeding from banging against the large rocks. For the sake of rescuing his son, the father enters into all the sufferings his son experiences for not having heeded his command. But it is only by diving into those same waters that the father is able to rise out of the river with his son and rescue him.

This is similar to what God does for us on the cross.

We turned away from God. And as a result, our sin has brought many sufferings into this world. We saw earlier how sin not only ruptures our relationship with God but also divides the human family: we have many hurts from the people

5   Augusta Theodosia Drane, *The History of St. Catherine of Siena and Her Companions* (London: Burns and Oates, 1880), 231.

around us. We also lost harmony with all of creation and now are exposed to many dangers, illnesses, and death. Because of sin, we live in this world with many fears, sorrows, hurts, and sufferings. But the greatest tragedy of all is that if we were left to ourselves, we would be eternally under the reign of the enemy and separated from God, the love we were made for.

But God doesn't leave us separated from him. Love impels God to dive into our world, to become one of us, to meet us in our sufferings and rescue us. This is what Jesus did throughout his public ministry. He constantly went out to the dark corners of Israel: to the poor, sick, suffering, and, most of all, those separated from God by sin. He is the Light of the World, who ardently longs to shine his light on all areas of sin, isolation, suffering, and darkness.

And this is what he did for us most fully on the cross. On Good Friday, Jesus entered the depths of our misery, the depths of the suffering that comes from sin. On Good Friday, he was misunderstood, unappreciated, mocked, rejected. His closest friends let him down that day. One even betrayed him. He was spit at, slapped, beaten, scourged, and nailed to the wood. But it wasn't just the intense physical suffering of crucifixion—that alone was horrific. It was also the sorrow, loneliness, and isolation—the feeling of being falsely accused and hated by the very people he came to save. In his passion and death, Jesus experienced the same sufferings we experience—the sufferings that plague this world because of our sin. On Good Friday, Jesus even descended into the depths of the ultimate curse, the great darkness that hangs over the human family: death.

And in so doing, Jesus was able to rise victoriously over death and free us from its chains. Like the father jumping into the river to save his son, Jesus entered fully into our sorrows to rescue us. Jesus took on the punishment, the curse of our sin—not primarily in the sense of an innocent person taking on the

severe punishment that someone else deserved but more in the
sense that he lovingly entered into the mess we made, the suffering we brought into the world through sin, so that he could
lead us out. Saint John Paul II explained it this way: what gives
Christ's death its "redemptive value is not the material fact that
an innocent person has suffered the chastisement deserved by
the guilty and that justice has thus been in some way satisfied".
Instead, its saving power "comes from the fact that the innocent
Jesus out of pure love, entered into solidarity with the guilty
and thus transformed their situation from within".[6]

The great medieval theologian Saint Anselm made a similar point. He explained the Cross not as an innocent person
volunteering to take the wrath and punishment of God that
should have been meted out on the guilty but as God compas-
sionately entering into our suffering and offering a gift of love.
Bishop Robert Barron summarizes Anselm's point like this:

> We sinners are like diamonds that have fallen into the muck;
> made in the image of God, we have soiled ourselves through
> violence and hatred. God ... could have simply pronounced
> a word of forgiveness from heaven, but this would not have
> solved the problem. It would not have restored the diamonds
> to their original brilliance. Instead, in his passion to reestab-
> lish the beauty of creation, God came down into the muck
> of sin and death and brought the diamonds up and polished
> them off. In so doing of course, God had to get dirty. This
> sinking into the dirt—this divine solidarity with the lost—is
> the "sacrifice" which the Son makes to the infinite pleasure
> of the Father. It is a sacrifice expressive, not of anger or ven-
> geance, but of compassion.[7]

6   John Paul II, General Audience, October 26, 1988, in *A Catechesis on the Creed*, vol. 2,
Jesus, Son and Savior (Boston: Pauline Books & Media, 1996), 445.
7   Robert Barron, *Heaven in Stone and Glass: Experiencing the Spirituality of the Great
Cathedrals* (New York: Crossroad, 2000), 44–45.

This is how much our God loves us. To rescue us, he jumped "into the muck of sin and death" and in the process "had to get dirty". He entered our suffering and death, but he did so not just because he wanted to rescue us, his precious diamonds in the muck. Rescuing us from eternal death is only one aspect of our salvation. God does even more. As we will see in the next chapter, he fills us with his life and transforms us, making us like him. In other words, God doesn't just overlook our sin and forgive us; he actually changes us and makes us new so that we sparkle with the radiance and love of God himself.

Reflection Questions:

1. How do the themes in this chapter change the way you think about the Cross?
2. Reflect on this concept from Saint Catherine of Siena about Jesus on Good Friday: the nails would not have held him to the cross if love had not held him there first. What does this tell you about Jesus' death for us on the cross?
3. Imagine being at Calvary. Jesus doesn't say a word, but he looks at you with love. You know that he went to the cross for you—not just for mankind in general, but for you personally. How would you feel at that moment? What would you say to Jesus? How do you think he would respond?

Chapter 7

Part 4: Re-Creation—
"I Make All Things New"

When an iron rod is placed in fire, what happens to it? It begins to take on the properties of fire. It becomes hot. It begins to glow red or orange. It starts to emit smoke. The iron rod doesn't become fire itself, but it starts to take on the characteristics of fire.

The same is true with our souls. When God fills us with his Spirit, our human nature is immersed in the fire of God's love, and we slowly become changed. We begin to love supernaturally—above and beyond what our human nature could do on its own. We begin to love like God loves, to be patient like he is patient, to be generous like he is generous, to sacrifice for others like he sacrifices for us. We begin to take on the characteristics of God as Christ's love transforms us. As Saint Paul explained, "It is no longer I who live, but Christ who lives in me" (Gal 2:20).

In this chapter, we will see that, in a sense, Jesus didn't die so we don't have to. He died and then rose and sent his Spirit into our hearts so that we could be changed—so that we could learn to love more like Jesus loved on the cross. He wants to reproduce his total, perfect, sacrificial love on the cross in our hearts. Describing this lifelong process of interior transformation, Saint Paul said, "Though our outer man is wasting away, our inner man is being renewed every day.... Therefore, if any one is in Christ, he is a new creation; the old has passed away, behold, the new has come" (2 Cor 4:16; 5:17).

Do you long for that renewal of your interior life—for that healing, that freedom, that transformation? Do you want God's love to change you like the fire transforms the iron rod? If you want the fullness of salvation Jesus offers, then you need the treasure of graces he makes available to you through his Church.

The Resurrection and the Life

This is the next key point of the Gospel message: God transforms us and makes us new. But before we reflect on this crucial aspect of our salvation, let's step back and recall the parts of the Gospel we've seen so far: God is love, and he made us to share in his love (part 1). Even though we turned away from his love in sin (part 2), God sought us out, became one of us, and offered his life on the cross as a gift of love on our behalf, reconciling us to himself (part 3). Jesus' death on Calvary— his total, perfect, sacrificial love—brings forgiveness of sins and restores us to a right relationship with the Father. How amazing God's love is! As Jesus himself said, "Greater love has no man than this, that a man lay down his life for his friends" (Jn 15:13).

Unfortunately, this is where many Christians stop when it comes to presenting the Gospel: *Jesus died for our sins.* That alone, of course, would be amazing! But Jesus came to do even more than that. He also rose from the dead! And by his Resurrection, he has set us free—free from sin, free from death, and free from the devil's hold on us. As Saint Augustine once said, "The dead Christ would be of no benefit to us unless he had risen from the dead."[1] But in rising from the dead, Jesus conquered death and freed us from the reign of the enemy. "He has delivered us from the dominion of darkness and transferred us to the kingdom of his beloved Son, in whom we have redemption, the forgiveness of sins" (Col 1:13–14).

But there's still more. The ultimate work Jesus does for our salvation takes place in our hearts. He rose from the dead, ascended into heaven, *and sent his Spirit into our hearts* (see Gal 4:6). Jesus pours his Spirit into our hearts so that we can be changed, so that he can relive his perfect, total, self-giving love—the love that he revealed on the cross—in us. In other words, the love Christ showed us on Good Friday isn't just something he did two thousand years ago. It's something he wants to reproduce in our hearts today. He wants to change our hearts so that we can love like he loves—so that we can be made new.

The Cross of Love

When I look at Jesus on the cross, I see such perfect love—such faithfulness, courage, generosity, and sacrifice. I see such patience, forgiveness, and mercy. I see Christ's total trust, surrendering himself completely to his heavenly Father.

But Jesus doesn't just want me to be in awe over his amazing love. He doesn't just want my gratitude or my applause. Ultimately, he wants my heart. He invites me to love like he loves. He wants to live his total, perfect, sacrificial love through me. Indeed, the Cross is not only the fullest revelation

---

1   Augustine, *Sermon* 246, 2 (PL 38, 1154), in *The Mystery of Jesus Christ* (Dublin: Four Courts Press, 1994), 164.

of God's love. It's also the fullest revelation of the love to which *we* are called. Jesus himself said, "Love one another as I have loved you" (Jn 15:12). This is the love we were made for. Indeed, it is only when we live like Christ—it is only when we live his total, self-giving love—that we will find our true happiness.

So, when I look at the Cross, I see not just the amazing love of God. I also see the high standard of love that God is revealing for *my* life. And in the process, I come to a greater awareness of the many ways I fall short of that beautiful love Jesus modeled for us on Good Friday. The contrasts are plentiful: Jesus remains faithful to me, even though I am not always faithful to him. Jesus is so generous with his life, giving everything, while I can be hesitant and selfish, holding back. Jesus has so much courage, sacrificing his entire life for us. But I get frustrated when small sufferings come my way and discouraged when things are hard.

When I look at the Cross, I see Jesus' patience with those who were persecuting him. His example challenges me to be more forbearing with the imperfection of others. I also see his mercy as he forgave those who nailed him to the cross, saying, "Father, forgive them; for they know not what they do" (Lk 23:34). Meanwhile, I can be tempted to hold on to resentments and not forgive from the heart.

When I look at the Cross, I see such trust, such dependance on the Father. Jesus' last words express his total surrender: "Father, into your hands I commit my spirit!" (23:46). I wish I trusted the Father like Jesus does. Too often, I'm afraid to put my life entirely into the Father's hands. I want to keep things in my hands. How often I fall into self-reliance, wanting to control and manage everything myself.

How about you? How well does your life reflect the love of Jesus on Good Friday? Do you notice areas where you can grow in order to reflect that total, perfect love of Christ more?

We all do, of course. But here we come to the height of the Good News. No matter how many ways you might fall short of loving like Christ loves, no matter what you've done, no matter how many times you've done it, no matter what you may be struggling with right now, no matter how many imperfections you think you need to overcome, Jesus came not only to forgive you, spare you from hell, and let you into heaven. He came to do so much more. He came to free you from whatever is keeping you from the fullness of his love. In other words, *Jesus doesn't just want to pardon you like a judge. He wants to heal you like a physician.* He wants to get to the *root* of your sins and heal you so that you can be changed and made new.

But some of us might be wondering, *Is this really possible? Can I really be changed? I have so many shortcomings. I'm far from being a saint. Such holiness and perfection are only for super holy people like Mother Teresa. I'm just an ordinary Catholic in pew 17. How can someone like me experience this transformation?*

Medicine

I have an amazing wife who always forgives me when my many weaknesses affect our relationship. Countless times throughout our marriage, she has forgiven me for my various faults and for the times I have hurt her. I am grateful for her tireless mercy.

But imagine if I were in a men's group sharing about my weaknesses and a friend in the group was a doctor. Imagine if that doctor said, "Did you know there's a new drug that can help you with all those struggles? If you take this medicine once a week, you'll be changed. It might take many months or even years, but over time, you will start to notice a difference. You'll gradually become more patient with your spouse, more generous, more honoring, more thankful, more sacrificial, humbler, and kinder. This new medication is really amazing!"

No doctor, of course, has a medicine like that. *But the Church does!* Jesus wants to heal us of our deepest weaknesses. And he does this through the sacraments, fellowship, and teachings of his Church. He wants to give us new hearts: to change our hard, selfish, fearful hearts into soft, generous, trusting hearts that take on the heart of Christ. This is what the prophet Ezekiel foretold: "A new heart I will give you, and a new spirit I will put within you; and I will take out of your flesh the heart of stone and give you a heart of flesh. And I will put my spirit within you, and cause you to walk in my statutes" (Ezek 36:26–27).

Grace: The Fire of God's Love

We definitely need new hearts! As we saw earlier, Original Sin didn't just separate us from God. It also left us with a deep wound in our souls. We have an inclination toward sin. It's not easy for us to do the good we know we should do. Recall Paul's description of our fallen human nature: "I do not understand my own actions. For I do not do what I want, but I do the very thing I hate.... For I do not do the good I want, but the evil I do not want is what I do" (Rom 7:15, 19).

How does God address this deep wound in our human nature? Does he just stand back and give us pardon from afar, while leaving us in this misery on the inside? No. He actually enters into our hearts and changes us from within so that we become healed of this wound. How does he do this? Through the power of his grace.

Christians talk about grace and even sing songs about how amazing it is. But what exactly is grace? Sanctifying grace is Christ's divine life in us. The supernatural life of Christ, the divine Son of God, is infused into our souls. "God has sent the Spirit of his Son into our hearts" (Gal 4:6). So we "become partakers of the divine nature" (2 Pet 1:4). In other words, we begin to share in the divine life of Christ and his perfect love, which changes us over time, making us more and more like him as we cooperate with those graces in our souls. Like the iron rod in the fire, our weak human nature, when filled with the fire of the Holy Spirit, becomes transformed. Through grace, we begin taking on the character of Christ and loving like he loves. As St. Paul said, "We ... are being changed into his likeness from one degree of glory to another" (2 Cor. 3:18). We first receive this grace at Baptism, and it grows in us through the other sacraments and the life of prayer and fellowship in Christ's Church.

The Church: Our Hospital

Think of the Church as the place of transformation. The Catholic Church is not a club of like-minded people who share similar values. Nor is the Church merely a way of life. It *is a life* that has been passed on from one generation to the next for two thousand years. Souls entering the Church at Baptism are immersed not just in water but in the divine life of Christ that comes to dwell in them. Indeed, the supernatural life of the Son of God dwells within us, healing us of our many weaknesses and enabling us to love with his love. *The Church, therefore, is not primarily a religious organization. It is a life—the life of Christ—that we share, bringing us true freedom and healing.*

We saw earlier how Saint Augustine, in his younger years, lived a wild life, searching for happiness in all the things of this world. But even though he reached a point of being intellectually convinced of the truth of Jesus, the Scriptures, and the Catholic Church, he held back and did not convert. To use a modern expression, we might say that for a period he was "spiritual but not religious". He came to believe in God and wanted to be a better man and change his sinful ways, but on his own, he could not find the strength to do so.

It was only when he finally converted to the Catholic faith that he found true freedom. The graces of the sacraments and the teachings of the Church gave him the strength and guidance to do what he could not do on his own. He finally became liberated from his sexual sins and committed his life to following Christ. This does not mean that everything became easy and that Augustine never again struggled with sin. Though he experienced a significant change when he entered the Church, his transformation continued for the rest of his life. As he later prayed to God, "It's not as though I do not suffer wounds, but I feel rather that you heal them over and over again."[2] That lifelong healing of Augustine's soul took place because of the treasures of grace available to him in the heart of Christ's Church.

A New Exodus

In the New Testament, the word Jesus used to describe his group of disciples was *ekklesia*. This Greek word is commonly translated "assembly" or "church", but it's based on two Greek words, *ek kalein*, which means "to call out of". It's a word used in the Old Testament to describe the Exodus story. God called the people of Israel out of slavery in Egypt and into freedom in the Promised Land. So, in Scripture, the word church—*ekklesia*—is, ultimately, a freedom word.

It's fascinating that this is what Jesus called his initial group of disciples; they were the *ekklesia*, those whom he *called out*

---

2   Augustine, *Confessions*, 10, 39.

of darkness and into light, out of slavery and into freedom. And that's what Jesus continues to do with his followers today through his Church. He calls us out of whatever sins, weaknesses, fears, addictions, and hurts keep us from his love. All that Jesus did for us on the cross is applied to our lives today through the Church. Indeed, it's through the Church that Christ heals and transforms us with his grace.

But some of us might think this amazing transformation is only for very holy people, like the saints, but is not possible for us. *I can't change. I will never be made holy. I have too many weaknesses and sins. I will never love like God loves. I can never be set free of my many faults.* If you have those thoughts in your head, they are not from God. It's the devil who wants us to believe those lies. From the very beginning, the devil tempted us, saying, in essence, "God doesn't want you to become like him." But that is the exact opposite of what God actually says. God *does* want to change us. He wants to make us new creations and give us new hearts. God's plan is for us "to be conformed to the image of [Christ]" (Rom 8:29), to be imitators of Christ (see 1 Cor 11:1), and even to be "changed into [Christ's] likeness" (2 Cor 3:18). This is what he has done for countless souls over the last two thousand years. He meets us in our weakness and really does transform us with his grace. And he gives us his grace most fully through his Church.

Earthen Vessels

Others of us might wonder how the Church could be the vessel of God's grace. The Church has so many problems. Many Catholics are not stellar models of Christianity. And many leaders in the Church are far from perfect. There have even been various scandals that have shaken the credibility of the

Catholic Church. Why would anyone want to entrust himself to a Church that's so imperfect?

This is a fair and important question. Saint Paul, however, reminds us that the treasure of grace—the grace that brings about this transformation in our souls—was never passed on through a perfect, utopian Church. Rather, he said, "We have this treasure in earthen vessels" (2 Cor 4:7). The heavenly graces Christ offers us have been passed on through weak, messy human vessels—communities, leaders, priests, bishops, and even popes who are far from perfect. That's the way it has been from the very beginning.

Think about it: Jesus himself chose twelve apostles. Were those twelve men models of perfection? Far from it! They were people like you and me—people with complicated problems and many faults. They fought with one another and misunderstood Jesus. They struggled with pride, selfishness, anger, and lack of trust. All but one abandoned Jesus on Good Friday. Peter, the leader of the Twelve, denied Jesus three times. And one of the apostles, Judas, even betrayed Jesus. So we can see that, from the start, Jesus chose to work through earthen vessels that were far from perfect. And yet he gave these imperfect, sinful men the authority to teach in his name, forgive sins, and bring healing to many souls (see Mt 10:1–40; Jn 20:19–22). He gave them authority to baptize people of all nations and promised that he would be with these apostles to the end of the age (see Mt 28:18–20). He even bestowed his own authority on these fallen men, saying, "He who hears you hears me, and he who rejects you rejects me" (Lk 10:16). And this authority has been passed on from the apostles to their successors, the bishops, from one generation to the next all the way down to the bishops we have today.

But imagine someone in the first century saying to Jesus, *I don't want to follow your apostles—they're not perfect like you. I just want to follow you.* Jesus would point out that to the extent we receive his apostles, we receive him, and if we reject his apostles, we reject him. Even though they were weak, imperfect earthen vessels, the treasure of graces is still passed on through them.

I personally find this encouraging. I'm grateful the Church isn't only for perfect people. If the Church were only for the perfect, there wouldn't be a place for me. I'm thankful Christ's Church is not a home only for those in the elite spiritual class of the faultless. I'm thankful it's more like a hospital, providing healing for ordinary souls who are deeply wounded, sick, and in need of a physician. Jesus is that Divine Physician, doing his deep work of healing for millions of souls like Augustine's. And he does this work through the sacraments, teachings, and fellowship found in the earthen vessel of the Catholic Church. It is Jesus through the Church (*ekklesia*) who *calls us out of* slavery to sin and calls us into the freedom found in his love.

Spiritual but Not Religious?

Still others in our modern world might ask, "Why do I need a Church? Can't I just be spiritual? I believe in God. I've got good values. I try to be nice to people. I'm spiritual but not religious. Why do I need a Church?"

I know myself. I know I need the Church. I need something outside myself calling me out of my complacency; calling me out of my tendency to pursue my own interests, comfort, pleasure, and gain; and calling me out of my propensity to fall short in the way I love others. I need what Christ's Church offers—*ek kalein*. I need to be *called out of* my selfishness and called to a greater love.

If I tried merely to be spiritual but not religious, I would end up creating spiritual and moral values that would be

comfortable for me. I would come up with a God who likes
all the things I like, loves all the things I love, hates all the
things I hate, and approves of all the things I approve of. But
similar to what we saw in chapter five, if I did that, who would
be made in the image of whom?[3] I would just be making a god
in my own image.

I can understand why being spiritual but not religious is
appealing in a world that wants to do its own thing. As I've
written elsewhere,

> It's easier to create my own religious and moral values—
> values that are comfortable to me—than it is to accept the
> revelation of Jesus Christ and the teachings of a Church that
> calls me to ongoing conversion. Rather than follow a moral
> standard outside myself—one that calls me on to greater re-
> sponsibility, commitment to others, generosity, and sacrificial
> love—I can determine for myself what is right and wrong. I
> can craft my own beliefs and values that conveniently justify
> my current way of living. In the world of being "spiritual but
> not religious", I can make myself my own pope in my own
> religion: the Church of Me.[4]

But I want much more than the Church of Me. I know
"me". I know that while I have some good qualities, I also
fall short in many ways in living the kind of love I'm made
for: the total, sacrificial love of Jesus on the cross. I know I
need *ekklesia*. I need Jesus calling me out of myself through
his Church. I need to be called *out of* myself and ever more
into Christ. That transformation in Christ happens most
fully through the Church. It is through the Church's sacraments that we receive Christ's grace and through the Church

---

3   Fr. Mike Schmitz, "What Jesus Teaches" (keynote address, SEEK23, January 3, 2023).
4   Edward Sri, *Love Unveiled: The Catholic Faith Explained* (San Francisco: Ignatius Press, 2015), 134–35.

that we receive the light of his revelation in its fullness. It is through the Church that we each are made "a new creation". It is through the Church that Jesus says to us, "Behold, I make all things new" (Rev 21:5).

Reflection Questions:

1. Recall the analogy of the iron rod being transformed by the fire. How might that analogy change the way you view holiness? How might it change the way you view your relationship with God?

2. Do you believe you can really be changed? That God has worked his transformation in countless souls who have gone before you, even souls that have had more problems, suffering, and sin than you do? What keeps you from entrusting your life more to Christ's healing power?

3. Recall how the word *Church* is rooted in the biblical word meaning "to call out of". What might Jesus, through his Church, be calling you out of right now?

4. We saw that Jesus carries out the transformation of our souls most fully through the teachings, sacraments, and fellowship found in his Church, the Catholic Church. How might this influence the way you view the Church? What are some practical ways you can welcome Jesus' healing power into your soul by receiving the truth, graces, and life of the Church more fully into your heart?

Chapter 8

Part 5: Response—"Follow Me"

When Jesus called his followers, he didn't instruct them to sign up for classes, register at the local synagogue, or sign a document stating their theological beliefs. Rather, he offered an invitation that was much more personal—something that would shape their entire lives. He said to them, "Follow me" (Mt 4:19; 8:22; 9:9; Mk 1:17; 2:14; Lk 5:27; 9:59; Jn 1:43).

In the first-century Jewish world of Jesus, these words would have signaled an invitation to become a disciple. The Greek word in the New Testament commonly translated "disciple" (*mathetes*) means "student" or "learner". But we shouldn't think of a student in a large lecture hall taking notes from a professor at a podium. While there was a lot of studying and memorizing involved, discipleship entailed so much more than scholarship. It shaped everything about the disciple's life.

If you were a disciple in Jesus' day, you would have a teacher, a "rabbi". But you didn't just listen to your rabbi's lectures on Mondays, Wednesdays, and Fridays and take good notes. You lived with your rabbi. You shared life with your rabbi. You shared meals with your rabbi, prayed with your rabbi, studied with your rabbi, and served the poor with your rabbi. Living day in and day out with your rabbi, you were immersed in his way of life. The goal was to follow not just your rabbi's teachings but also the way he lived. As Jesus himself said, "A disciple is not above his teacher, but every one when he is fully taught will be like his teacher" (Lk 6:40).

That's the goal of our discipleship: to follow our rabbi, Jesus—to immerse ourselves in his way of life and ultimately become like him. As he did with those original disciples, Jesus says to us today, "Follow me." And how we answer that call makes all the difference in our lives.

If we say yes, it will shape every aspect of who we are, not just what we do on Sunday. Following Jesus is not simply about going to Mass each week, volunteering at the parish, and putting money in the collection basket. It's also not merely about saying some prayers, taking in good Catholic content, and participating in good Catholic activities. And it's even more than just believing the right things, saying the right things, and doing the right things.

All that is very good, of course. Indeed, attending Mass, praying, and following all the teachings of Christ are absolutely essential. But following the rules and believing the right things alone doesn't make someone a great Christian disciple. It is just the starting point. Being a true follower of Jesus involves much more than checking off all the right Catholic boxes. It's more about what's happening on the inside. We can go through all the external motions of the faith but not be true disciples of Jesus. Are we willing to give Jesus everything?

Total Commitment

The biblical word for conversion is *metanoia*—a Greek word that literally means "to turn or turn around". The idea is that a person reorients his life around God. He turns away from sin and turns back toward God. He shifts his priorities in life from seeking things like success, praise, wealth, and pleasure to putting Christ first and at the very center of all he does. In fact, when the Catholic Church teaches about the journey of discipleship, it describes this conversion as someone "surrendering" his life to Christ, "saying yes" to Jesus, becoming "fervent in faith and Christian living". It's a reorientation of one's entire life around Christ, seeking first his will and his kingdom.

This is what we see with those original disciples Jesus called two thousand years ago. When Jesus' disciples answered the call to follow him, it was a life-shaping decision. They left a former way of life behind and entered a new way of life in Christ. And they were changed. Matthew left his money bags behind at the tax collector's office. Peter and Andrew dropped their fishing nets. James and John left their father's business. And these men, who gave up everything and followed Jesus, were changed. Over time—and even through many mistakes, setbacks, and trials—they were transformed. They became saints reflecting the love of Jesus himself.

Others, however, chose *not* to answer Christ's call. Some were interested in Jesus but hesitated. They had other priorities in life, so they put off the decision and said no (see Mt 8:18–22). Others started following him but didn't like his teaching, so they eventually chose to leave him (see Jn 6:60). Still others, like the Pharisees, had even harder hearts and were opposed to Jesus from the very beginning.

There also were many who liked Jesus for what he did for them—he was an inspiring preacher, performed many miracles, and helped people with their problems. But they were like the crowds who merely wanted Jesus to multiply more loaves and feed them. They liked what Jesus could do for them but did not understand who he really was and refused to follow him (see Jn 6). There were even some, like the rich young man, who sincerely sought eternal life and obeyed all the commandments but were unwilling to give up everything to follow Christ. They were too attached to their own plans and possessions (see Mt 19:16–22).

These are not just stories from a long time ago. They are included in the Gospels to invite us to examine our own hearts. We can put ourselves in the scenes and imagine Jesus calling us today: "Follow me." How would you respond? Would you say yes like Peter, Andrew, James, and John? Or would you be among those who put off the decision and missed the moment of God's call in their lives?

Would you be like the crowds who came to Jesus primarily because of what he did for them, treating God like a spiritual Santa Claus who solves your problems and helps you get what you want in life? Or do you lovingly seek God for his own sake, striving to use your life for his purposes and not your own?

Are you willing to entrust everything in your life to God's hands, truly putting God first in your life? Or would you walk away like the rich young man because, deep down, you know you have other priorities and certain plans for your life that you think you must absolutely cling to in order to be happy?

To be clear, most of us probably won't be called to quit our jobs, sell our belongings, and leave our homes like those original disciples did. But there may be other things Jesus invites us to leave behind: our attachment to being liked, an unhealthy need to win certain people's approval, a harbored resentment against someone, a desire to control everything, an unhealthy relationship, a certain plan for our career, a show we watch that has images a Christian should not put before his eyes. Indeed, we are all called to an ever-deeper conversion— turning away from whatever keeps us from a deeper union with Jesus.

Ongoing Conversion

Conversion is not just a one-time event. Rather, it's something that is meant to be ongoing throughout our lives. A true disciple is always seeking new ways to turn away from self and turn more toward God.

It's true that some Christians speak about a foundational conversion moment in their lives—a certain point or season of life when they made a firm commitment to turn away from sin and follow Christ. But that commitment to Jesus is meant to be renewed and deepened over and over.

Consider the example of the Blessed Virgin Mary. She gave her foundational fiat when she said Yes to the angel's message and surrendered to God's plan for her life. That initial fiat certainly was a crucial step in her discipleship. But, as Saint John Paul II explained, she had to renew her fiat countless times in her life. God continued to invite her to take further steps in faith—to give more, trust more, surrender more, and sacrifice more. And he does the same with us.

That's why the topic we're about to explore next is so important, not just for souls who are new to the Catholic faith, but for all committed Catholics as well. We might be going through all the motions of the faith: going to Mass on Sundays, participating in various parish activities, trying to obey God's commandments. But maybe we have never really encountered Jesus in a personal way—his love, his mercy forgiving us, his grace upholding us.

Maybe the Gospel message we've been considering in this book is new to us. Or, even if we have heard these ideas before, perhaps we've never really internalized them. We've never allowed them to penetrate our hearts deeply and shape our daily lives. Maybe we've never committed to follow Jesus as disciples, saying yes to him, making a decisive choice to turn away from sin, and surrendering our lives to his plan.

Or, even if we might be able to point to a conversion moment in our past (a retreat, a time in prayer, a certain period when our faith life took off), perhaps we have not renewed our personal encounter with Christ in a long time. And as the years have passed, we have started to lose the initial fervor of our faith. If we're honest, we realize we are not seeking Jesus like we used to—we are not on the lookout for the new ways Jesus is inviting us to turn away from sin, love him more, trust him more, and follow him more. We have become comfortable in our walk with God, holding back in our generosity. We are just coasting in our faith life and not really seeking ongoing conversion anymore. Fr. Donald Hagerty explains that we must be on guard against any lukewarmness that creeps into our relationship with Christ. "There is a deeper interior dimension in a personal love for Our Lord that awaits our soul.... We have to sense an invitation after a certain point in life to risk everything and even life itself by means of a free, unconstrained offering to God. Only then, perhaps can God truly do as he wants with us, with no question or objection from our part. Otherwise, the effort of love tends to settle down into paced and manageable generosity, undergoing the same aging and stiffening with the years as our body."[1]

Whatever situation we might find ourselves in, Jesus continues to say the same two words to us all: "Follow me." His loving invitation is always present. He wants us to encounter him anew. A true disciple should always be considering how to answer that call: *What is the next step of faith God is inviting me to take? How is he inviting me to a deeper conversion? How is he calling me to love more like he loves? What sins and*

---

1   Donald Hagerty, *Conversion* (San Francisco: Ignatius Press, 2017), 154.

bad habits is he calling me to turn away from now? How is he inviting me to trust him more? How is he inviting me to a deeper union with him?

What True Conversion Really Looks Like

The Parable of the Prodigal Son beautifully shows us what true conversion looks like. But get ready. There's a lot more to the story than we may initially realize—a lot that challenges us to see how deep of conversion wants for our souls.

In this famous parable, Jesus tells about a father who has two sons. The younger son carries out a series of actions that, especially in the first-century Jewish world, would have been utterly shocking. First, he asks for his inheritance—which is usually given only when the father dies. Nevertheless, this younger son demands his inheritance even while his father is still living. In doing so, the son is basically saying, *I wish you were dead.... This inheritance is much more important to me than you are!*

But it gets even worse. The son does the unthinkable. He sells his inheritance, his portion of the family land. In the ancient biblical mindset, the family's land was supposed to be passed on from one generation to the next. It was the *family's* land across the generations, not any one family member's private possession. Many ancestors before him had taken care of the land so that he could receive its blessings. And it was his turn now to care for it so that descendants after him could receive its blessings as well. But in one foolish, selfish act, he sold the family's land and squandered it on prostitutes.

The younger son certainly has a lot of sins he needs to turn away from: rejecting the father, selling the family land, indulging in immoral sexual behavior, treating women like objects to be used. Thankfully, he comes to his senses, decides to leave that life behind, and returns to his father. This is the foundational level of conversion: turning away from sin.

But there's more. There's a second kind of conversion he still needs to undergo.

"I Am Not Worthy"

As the story progresses, we learn that the younger son plans to go home and tell his father, "I have sinned against heaven and before you; I am no longer worthy to be called your son; treat me as one of your hired servants" (Lk 15:18–19). He feels so ashamed. In his mind, he has done too much harm. He doesn't think he can be truly forgiven. And any hope of being welcomed back into the family is completely out of the question. After all he has done, the best he can hope for is to be treated as an employee, a hired servant. He thinks he is not worthy of the father's love.

But the father will have none of this. When the son returns and begins his words of self-reproach, the father cuts him off. As soon as the young man says, "I am no longer worthy to be called your son" (15:19), the father interrupts him. He won't let his son complete his statement of self-condemnation or even speak of being treated as a hired servant. Instead, the father has the best robe brought out for him and the prized fatted calf killed, and he holds a feast to welcome his son home. No matter what the son has done, one thing has remained the same all these years: his son is always his son. "This my son was dead, and is alive again; he was lost, and is found" (15:24).

We see here that the father's love is stronger than any of the horrific sins the son committed. In fact, the parable gives two small details that point to this amazing love. First, while the son is still at a distance, the father sees him coming. This points to how, all along, the father had been lovingly looking, waiting, yearning for this moment—always longing for his son to return. And a second detail reveals the father's love even more. At the first glimpse of his son coming in the distance, the father *runs* to meet him. In the first-century Jewish culture, an older man walked deliberately, in a dignified way. For the father to *run* toward his son, therefore, would have been a most unexpected sight. But his running to his son reveals his heart. Indeed, the father's love for his son impels him to throw off all custom and worldly honor. None of that matters now. The father runs to embrace his son and welcome him back home.

The younger son's conversion, therefore, not only entails his turning away from sin. It also involves his turning away from the false view he had of himself. He viewed himself as unworthy of the father's love. He saw himself trapped by his past, by his many failures and sins. He thought that those sins must continue to define him; that he is unforgivable, unlovable, and unworthy; that he has no hope of being free from his past; that he has no hope in being a son again, living in his father's love.

His conversion also entails his turning away from the way he saw his father: that his father had rejected him, that his father had forgotten him and abandoned him, that his father's love was beyond him. From a human perspective, that's what one would expect—that the father would disown the son. But the younger son comes to know the father in a new way. He comes to know the heart of his father. He comes to experience the father's total, unconditional love—a love he doesn't deserve, but a love that nonetheless is generously and freely given to him.

And still, there's more to the story that points to a third level of conversion.

A Transactional Relationship

The last part of the parable focuses on the other son: the older brother. As we will see, this son also needs conversion. The older brother is upset that the younger brother came home to such a warm reception. He's angry and refuses to celebrate his brother's return. He says to his father, "Behold, these many years I have served you, and I never disobeyed your command; yet you never gave me a kid, that I might make merry with my friends. But when this son of yours came, who has devoured your living with harlots, you killed for him the fatted calf!" (15:29–30).

The older brother had done everything right. He had been faithful. He was disciplined. He did what he was told. He didn't dishonor his father, sell the property, and live an immoral life. The older brother was obedient. But he thinks he has to do all these things to earn his father's approval and win the blessings he has to offer. He has a transactional relationship with his father. He can feel good about himself by controlling his performance: doing the right things, saying the right things, believing the right things. Yet the father wants so much more than his son's obedience, as important as that is. He, ultimately, wants his son's heart. He wants his son to know his love—to know that his love is freely given, that there is nothing he can do to earn the father's love or lose it, that he is beloved not for what he does but for who he is as his son. The father says to him, "Son, you are always with me, and all that is mine is yours" (15:31).

Which Son Are You?

Which son do you identify with more—the younger or the older?

As with the younger son, perhaps there's a certain area of our lives that is not aligned with God's commandments, a sin we need to repent of and bring to Confession. For example, a selfish neglect of the poor and suffering around us, a hard heart that judges other souls, an intentional skipping of Mass on Sundays, hurtful words we tend to say, an ungrateful heart that criticizes and complains, use of pornography or other sexual sin, a marriage situation that needs to be reconciled with the Church. The younger son had certain behaviors he needed to change, and so do we. Will we repent, go to Confession, and receive the Father's mercy?

Or perhaps there's a wound in our lives that keeps Jesus' loving mercy from reaching the depths of our hearts: shame, self-hatred, self-condemnation, a sin from the past that we think can't be forgiven. We think we will never be able to break free and change. We think we are unworthy of God's love. Like the younger son, we might have a false way of viewing our relationship with the Father: We don't realize how merciful, patient, and eager to forgive God is and how much his grace can free us from whatever weaknesses or sins keep us from his love. We need to see our sins and failures the way the Father sees them. Like the father in the parable, our heavenly Father is looking on the horizon for us, longing for us to return. When we come back to him, he's not pointing fingers, counting our sins, or reprimanding us for taking so long to get our act together. Like the father in the story, God is running out to us with his arms open wide. He is not condemning. He's eager to remove whatever obstacles are keeping us from union with him. And once he sees our repentant heart—that we are truly sorry, that we are turning away from sin and back to his love—he rushes to welcome us home. Our conversion isn't just turning away from sin but also turning away from self-condemnation and the false images we have of God: from not trusting in the Father's love; from thinking we cannot be forgiven; from not believing that God can free us from our sins and addictions; from thinking we have to rely on ourselves to fix all our faults and failures.

Or maybe we are like the older brother: we exteriorize our faith, making it primarily about how much we know and understand, what prayers we recite, what sins we avoid, and what good Catholic activities we pursue. We seek our identity in what we accomplish in the spiritual life—our devotions, self-discipline, and sacrifices—instead of experiencing the love of God as freely given. Like the older brother, we don't see ourselves as beloved children. Rather, we approach our relationship with God in a transactional way: we have to do certain things to please the Father and earn his love. And perhaps there might be some self-centered motive lurking behind our outward Catholic lifestyle: if we check off all the boxes and go through all the external motions of the faith, it makes us feel good about ourselves. Like the older brother, we do what we are told, so we must be good sons and daughters.

But just because we live our faith correctly in all the practices the Church requires doesn't mean we are facing the deeper weaknesses and wounds in our souls that keep us from experiencing the fullness of the Father's love. Just because we pray the right prayers, listen to the right podcasts, participate in the right kind of liturgy, sing the right kind of music, and believe all the right doctrines does not necessarily mean we are allowing ourselves to encounter the Father in our poverty—in those many areas where we don't have it all together—which is precisely where he wants us to experience his love the most and learn to rely on him to do what we can't do on our own.

God doesn't want us just to follow rules, as important as those rules may be. Ultimately, he wants our hearts. He wants to heal and transform our hearts at the deepest levels. Remember the iron rod in the fire analogy. God wants to transform the iron rod of our weak, selfish human hearts with the fire of his Holy Spirit. He wants to make us new.

To be sure, taking an honest look at our souls can be scary. It's not easy to face the truth about ourselves—our many faults, fears, insecurities, areas of selfishness, hurts from the past, anxieties in the present, and agitated desires to control everything in the future. It's easier to focus on all the externals—all the right answers and all the minimum requirements of the faith—than it is to face the reality of how little we are in control of our lives, how selfish we really are, how much we are tempted to sin, and how much we need God. We wish we didn't have to depend on the Lord and rely on his mercy so much. We are afraid of accepting our littleness. But this kind of fear, no matter how much it is disguised by our outwardly correct practice of the faith, can lead to a dangerous self-sufficiency and spiritual pride. It can become another way the devil gets us to turn away from the Father's love, like the older brother did. This is the third level of conversion God invites us to.

The Parable of the Prodigal Son has it all: Sin. Rebellion. Fear. False images of God. False stories we tell about ourselves. Spiritual pride. These are the various obstacles that keep the two sons in the parable from receiving the father's love. And they are the kinds of obstacles that prevent us from encountering God today. When Jesus calls us to follow him, he invites us to leave all these obstacles behind so that his love can more fully fill our hearts.

How might Jesus be inviting you to follow him more closely? What might Jesus be asking *you* to turn away from?

Not Perfect, but Chosen

But what if we're not perfect yet? How could we possibly follow Jesus as his disciples?

We might say to ourselves, *I'm not like all those fervent Chris-*
tians out there. I have too many problems—too many weaknesses
and sins. I'm not good at prayer and don't know enough about
the Catholic faith. I'm not ready to follow Christ as a disciple.

That's exactly what the devil wants us to think. He wants
us to think we have to fix all our problems before we become
disciples. But with self-reliance we'll never succeed. The truth
is that we need Jesus. We need Jesus to help us do what we
can't do on our own.

Think about it: Did Jesus wait for those first disciples to reach
perfection before he called them? They were sinners with many
weaknesses, just like you and me. They struggled with pride,
envy, anger, selfishness. They often didn't understand what
Jesus was teaching. They fought with one another. Even after
three years of intense training, most of them failed miserably
on Good Friday, abandoning Jesus in his greatest hour of need.
These men were not expected first-round draft picks for Jesus'
kingdom-building team. They were far from perfect. They were
works in progress. Yet, even though they didn't come with ideal
spiritual resumes, Jesus called them, and they answered the call
and sincerely *tried* to follow him as disciples.

Could you do that much? Could you commit to sincerely
trying to follow Jesus the best you can? If you stumble along
the way, don't worry. Those original apostles did as well. They
(and countless saints throughout the ages) often fell. But each
time they fell, they always got up and tried again, learning
ever more to rely on Jesus' mercy and grace. And, over time,
they were changed.

That's a path of discipleship within our reach. That's a path
all of us can follow. You don't have to be a superhero Christian with extraordinary spiritual powers to be a disciple. And
you certainly don't have to be perfect to begin following Jesus.
Indeed, Jesus doesn't call the perfect. He tells us he came not
for the healthy but for the sick who are in need of a physician

(see Mt 9:12; Mk 2:17; Lk 5:31). And we all have a long list of maladies that need his healing. We might be tempted to think we have to get our lives in order before we begin following Christ. But the truth is just the opposite: We need to begin following Christ, so that we can allow *him* to get our lives in order. In fact, we can't fix ourselves. Like those initial disciples, we can experience deep transformation only when we step out and begin to follow Jesus. He alone can free us from the sins enslaving us and fill us with his Spirit to change our hearts.

"Be Not Afraid"

But what if we are nervous about committing our lives to Christ and following him as disciples? What if we are afraid of changing, letting go of our own will and abandoning ourselves to him?

First, think about who is making this invitation, who is saying to us, "Follow me." This is Jesus, the God-man. This is the God who is love, the God who made you out of love so that you can share in his love. And even though you have turned away from him in sin, he still seeks you out. This is how much he loves you. He thirsts for you. He longs for your heart, your time, your attention. He loves you so much he entered your world, became fully human, and even offered up his life as a gift of love for you. As we saw earlier, Love is a Person, a Person who died for you. It is Love who is making this invitation: "Follow me."

Still, entrusting our lives to Christ might seem scary at first. It might mean making changes in the way we live. It might involve giving up a certain sin or reprioritizing how we spend our time and what we run after in life to make more space in our hearts for God. We might be afraid to make Jesus' prayer in Gethsemane our own: "Not my will, but yours, be done" (Lk 22:42). As Pope Benedict once explained,

> Are we not perhaps all afraid in some way? If we let Christ enter fully into our lives, if we open ourselves totally to him, are we not afraid that He might take something away from us? Are we not perhaps afraid to give up something significant, something unique, something that makes life so beautiful? Do we not then risk ending up diminished and deprived of our freedom?

To all these fears, Pope Benedict answered emphatically,

> No! If we let Christ into our lives, we lose nothing, nothing, absolutely nothing of what makes life free, beautiful and great. No! Only in this friendship are the doors of life opened wide. Only in this friendship is the great potential of human existence truly revealed. Only in this friendship do we experience beauty and liberation. And so, today, with great strength and great conviction, on the basis of long personal experience of life, I say to you, dear young people: Do not be afraid of Christ! He takes nothing away, and he gives you everything. When we give ourselves to him, we receive a hundredfold in return. Yes, open, open wide the doors to Christ—and you will find true life.[2]

Open Wide the Doors to Christ

Jesus stands at the door of our hearts. He knocks. Will we let him in? Will we open wide the doors to Jesus Christ? God

2   Benedict XVI, homily, April 24, 2005, https://www.vatican.va/content/benedict-xvi/en/homilies/2005/documents/hf_ben-xvi_hom_20050424_inizio-pontificato.html.

meets us wherever we may be in our faith life. He calls us. He says, "Follow me." How will we respond?

One way to put into practice this desire to open wide the doors to Christ is to tell Jesus that we want to follow him, that we commit our lives to seeking him and his will. As Catholics, we have many opportunities to reaffirm and rekindle our faith in Christ—at Mass, in the sacraments, in the Creed, in renewing our baptismal promises. But one other simple and powerful way we can renew our commitment to Christ is by offering a prayer of surrender—a simple prayer in which we place our entire life in God's hands. It's a prayer that expresses our desire to open wide the doors to Christ—to put him first in our lives and follow him as disciples. It's something many saints have done in different ways. And it's something ordinary people like you and me can do as well. Indeed, even if we have offered a prayer like this in the past, we can and should renew our personal commitment to Christ regularly.

One prayer of surrender from the Catholic tradition was written by the sixteenth-century Saint Ignatius of Loyola. You can take a moment right now to pray this beautiful prayer, found at the end of the chapter. But, to be clear, no private prayer on its own is a magical wand that suddenly makes someone a disciple and quickly transforms him in holiness. And we certainly need the Church and the sacraments—and most especially the Sacrament of Reconciliation—to turn away from sin and encounter the Father's mercy throughout our journey of ongoing conversion. Nevertheless, telling the Lord we love him, entrusting our entire lives to him, and telling him that we want to seek his will above all things is a beautiful gift of ourselves that we can give to the Lord. Like Mary, we give the Lord our hearts. We give him our personal fiat. Like Mary, we affirm to God that we are here to serve him. Like Mary, we surrender to his plan for our lives, not our own. Like Mary, we say, "Let it be to me according to your word" (Lk 1:38).

Whether this is your first time entrusting your life to God—giving him your own fiat—or whether you are renewing a commitment you made to Jesus long ago, a prayer of surrender is a powerful way to express your desire to follow Jesus as a disciple, to seek him first above all things, and to use your life not for your own purposes but for God's.

So, at the culmination of these reflections on the Gospel, I invite you not just to *read* this prayer from Saint Ignatius like you've been reading the rest of this book. Rather, I invite you to *pray* it from your heart—to speak these words with love to your God who so loves you, giving your life to him, who gave his life for you. We were made for this love. Indeed, it is only when we give our lives away in love to God that we find our true happiness, salvation, and eternal life.

> Take, Lord, receive all my liberty.
> My memory, my understanding, my entire will.
> All that I have and possess.
> You have given all to me. To you I return them.
> All is yours. Dispose of them according to your will.
> Give me only your love and your grace.
> With these I am rich enough and wish for nothing more.
> —Suscipe Prayer of Saint Ignatius[3]

Reflection Questions:

1. Which of the following scenarios best describes your relationship with Jesus right now?
   • Jesus is not a part of my life. Not important to me at all.

---

3   St. Ignatius of Loyola, *Spiritual Exercises*, trans. Louis J. Puhl, SJ (Chicago: Loyola University Press, 1951), 102.

- Jesus is a *part* of my life. Important, but honestly just one of many things.
- Jesus is at the *very center* of my life. The most important part and motivation for all I do.

2. Do you want a closer friendship with Christ? If so, what would it take to put him more at the center of your life?

Moving Forward:
The Four Habits of a Disciple

Whether this is the first time you have said yes to Jesus or you are renewing and deepening your personal encounter with Christ, there are four key habits every disciple needs if he desires to grow in his relationship with Christ.

These four habits, however, are not based on one author's creative ideas about discipleship. Rather, they come right from the inspired Word of God and the heart of the Catholic Church. These four habits are found in Acts of the Apostles, shortly after the scene of Pentecost. The Bible tells us the earliest disciples committed themselves to these four practices: prayer, the breaking of the bread, fellowship, and the teachings of the apostles.

So important were these four practices that when the Church wanted to sum up the Catholic faith, it has often turned to these four areas. In fact, the *Catechism of the Catholic Church* beautifully reflects this tradition with its four main sections known as the four pillars of the *Catechism*: the Creed (the teachings of the apostles), the sacraments (the breaking of the bread), the moral life (living in fellowship with one another and with God), and prayer.

First, we want to cultivate the habit of daily *prayer*. The soul needs prayer like the body needs oxygen. We, therefore, want to take in the deep breath of prayer each day. This is more than just saying vocal prayers like the Our Father or praying devotions like the Rosary. These, of course, are very good. But a disciple also needs time in quiet prayer each day, in what the Church calls meditation. This involves reflecting on a sacred text like Scripture or the writing of a saint or perhaps using a devotional book that can guide our meditation. Whatever form or methods of prayer we use, the crucial point is that we take time—at least fifteen to thirty minutes—each day to reflect on God's Word, listen to God, and talk with him.

Second, we need to develop the habit of *frequenting the sacraments* (the breaking of the bread). And here we focus on the two sacraments we can encounter regularly: the Eucharist and Confession. The Eucharist is not just a symbol of Jesus. It is the Real Presence of Jesus under the appearance of bread and wine. When we receive Holy Communion, we are receiving God himself into our souls. Communion is the most intimate union we can have with God in this life. So, while going to Mass each Sunday (and holy days of obligation) is the minimal requirement, we might want to consider going to Mass during the week if that's possible. The Eucharist strengthens us, helps us overcome sin, heals our weaknesses, and brings us into deeper union with Christ and one another. Everyone's circumstances are different, and the ability to participate in a weekday Mass will depend on each person's situation. But if we want a deeper communion with Jesus, with our spouse, with our children, with our friends, and with all our brothers and sisters in Christ, we should at least long to receive Holy Communion as often as we can.

Similarly, though the Church requires only that we go to Confession once a year at minimum, a true disciple should long for the Sacrament of Reconciliation often. Going regularly, about once a month, is a good practice to develop. After all, most of us have more than enough sins to bring to Confession in one month's time! Some of the great saints went every day. The Sacrament of Reconciliation doesn't just bring forgiveness of sins. It also brings graces to help us overcome our sins. So if we want to get to the roots of our sins and experience the healing power of God more in our lives, we should want to frequent the Sacrament of Reconciliation.

Third, we need *Christian fellowship*. Having good Christian friendships is crucial for growing in our faith life. Think of a campfire: a piece of wood placed near other burning logs will catch on fire. But if that same piece of wood is removed from the campfire, it will begin to lose its flame. Similarly, we need to be around other burning logs to keep the flame of faith growing in us. If we become isolated, it will be a lot harder to keep our faith alive, especially in a secular culture surrounded by people who do not have the same Christian vision for life. We also are called to love Christ in the people around us— whether it's a spouse, a child, a colleague, a friend, or the poor, the suffering, and the lonely in this world. Living in community with others gives us many opportunities to love like Jesus loves. We encounter Jesus not just in prayer and in the sacraments but also in our neighbor.

Fourth, we need to form our minds with *the teachings of the apostles* handed on to us through the Church. Saint Paul gave important advice to the Christians living in a pagan culture that often had values and lifestyles that undermined the Christian life. He said, "Do not be conformed to this world but be transformed by the renewal of your mind" (Rom 12:2). He emphasized how important it is to form our minds with the truth revealed by Jesus Christ. In our non-Christian age, we have to realize there's a battle for our minds. What we put in our minds matters. It shapes our imagination, what we perceive as good, and our desires. So, if we fill our minds more with shows, music, videos, sports, and other content from our secular world than we do with the Word of God, we will end up being conformed to this world more than to Christ. A Christian disciple, therefore, wants to make sure he is filling his mind regularly with the Scriptures, the writings of the saints, Church teachings, and other resources that support our Catholic faith.

Prayer, sacraments, fellowship, and the teachings of the apostles. These are the four foundational practices we need to follow Jesus as true disciples. Think of these four habits as places of continued encounter. They are not merely items to get done on a good Catholic to-do list. Rather, these are the primary ways we renew our encounter with Christ in our daily lives. Jesus wants us to encounter him in daily prayer and in the sacraments. He also wants us to meet him in our neighbor and in his teachings. Indeed, these are the very places where Jesus does his work of transformation in our souls. Jesus says, "I came that they may have life, and have it abundantly" (Jn 10:10). That abundant life in Christ is deepened through living these four habits throughout our lives as we follow Jesus as his disciples.

Reflection Questions:

1. This chapter focused on the four habits of a disciple from Acts 2:42: prayer, sacraments, fellowship, and forming our minds with the teaching of the apostles. Which of these habits do you think God is inviting you to grow in most right now?
2. What can you do this week to begin putting that habit into practice?
3. Of the many topics covered in this book, which insight moved you the most? Why?

Acknowledgments

I am grateful to Curtis Martin and various FOCUS missionaries for conversations about how to share the Gospel message effectively in the modern age. Those discussions over the last twenty-five years have deepened my own understanding of the kerygma and the way I teach it in the classroom and share it with others. I am thankful for conversations with Lucas Pollice and Ben Akers, who have helped develop my thought on how to present some points of the kerygma in a parish catechetical setting.

I am also grateful to Father Joseph Fessio, S.J., Mark Brumley, Ben Akers, and Carrie Wagner for reviewing parts of the manuscript and for their helpful suggestions. Thanks also goes to Diane Eriksen and the Ignatius Press editorial team for their recommendations that helped make this a better book and to Shannon Hicks, Carrie Wagner, Megan Ferowich, and Sabrina Sanchez for their creative ideas that led to the book's title.

Finally, I thank my wife, Beth, for her prayers and support for me in this project and for her helpful insights on parts of the book.

About the Author

Dr. Edward Sri is a theologian, author, and well-known Catholic speaker. Each year he presents to clergy, parish leaders, catechists, and laity from around the world.

He has written several best-selling books, including *The Art of Living* (Augustine Institute–Ignatius Press); *Who Am I to Judge? Responding to Relativism with Logic and Love* (Augustine Institute–Ignatius Press); *Men, Women, and the Mystery of Love* (Servant); *A Biblical Walk through the Mass* (Ascension); and *Walking with Mary* (Image).

Dr. Sri is also the host of the acclaimed film series *Symbolon: The Catholic Faith Explained* (Augustine Institute) and the presenter of several popular faith-formation programs, including *A Biblical Walk through the Mass* (Ascension) and *Mary: A Biblical Walk with the Blessed Mother* (Ascension).

He is a founding leader with Curtis Martin of FOCUS (Fellowship of Catholic University Students), where he currently serves as senior vice president of Apostolic Outreach. Dr. Sri is also the host of the weekly podcast *All Things Catholic* and leads pilgrimages to Rome and the Holy Land each year. He holds a doctorate from the Pontifical University of St. Thomas Aquinas in Rome and is a visiting professor at the Augustine Institute. He and his wife, Elizabeth, have eight children and reside in Littleton, Colorado. You can connect with Dr. Sri through his website, www.edwardsri.com, or follow him on Instagram, Facebook, and Twitter.